Rail Routes in
DEVON & CORNWALL

Previous page: **The Class 25 diesel locomotives have now gone from the West Country, but on 10 July 1976 No 25.223 was at Barnstaple on the 13.40 arrival from Exeter St Davids. The former Barnstaple Junction station is now the only survivor of the town's three stations.** *Brian Morrison*

Below: **Westbound trains seen at Newton Abbot on a Saturday afternoon in July 1959.** *D. S. Fish*

Rail Routes in
DEVON & CORNWALL

Chris Leigh

LONDON
IAN ALLAN LTD

Contents

First published 1982

ISBN 0 7110 1184 2

Published by Ian Allan Ltd, Shepperton, Surrey; and printed by Ian Allan Printing Ltd at their works at Coombelands in Runnymede, England

Right: Calstock viaduct is the major civil engineering feature of the PD&SWJR line. On 15 July 1980 the Plymouth-based two-car dmu which seems to monopolise the branch services, meanders high above the Tamar with the 12.00 Gunnislake-Plymouth.
Brian Morrison

Introduction

The current rail system in Devon and Cornwall reflects the problems that have faced Britain's railways since the war. Rising costs, competition from alternative forms of transport and the consequent falling numbers of passengers have led to considerable reductions to the network that had been built up since the 19th century. A comparison between the maps of the network in 1948 and 1981 illustrates the change graphically. The Beeching cuts and subsequent rationalisation have left areas of the countryside — especially North Cornwall — bereft of rail transport. Those lines that remain — primarily the Western Region's main line to Penzance from Paddington, its branches, and the Southern Region's Waterloo-Exeter service — fulfil more economically the needs of an area noted for its scenic qualities and large seasonal tourist traffic. Little remains of the myriad branch lines that grew up in the 19th century, except for some freight only lines — particularly those serving the China clay industry — and today's traveller has to use car or bus to get away from the better known areas.

Rail Routes in Devon and Cornwall does not attempt to describe the history of the railways in the two counties in detail, although a short history section records some of the now defunct branch lines. The emphasis of the book is on the existing network — what it looks like today and what can be seen on it — and the changes effected by the appearance of diesel motive power and rebuilding. To this end the photographs have been chosen for their atmosphere rather than a direct statement of facts and it is hoped that the visitor to the counties or, indeed, the railway enthusiast in situ, will find the book a useful companion as he travels the rail routes of Devon and Cornwall.

Chris Leigh
Simon Forty
Alan Butcher

Historic Routes

The early history of Britain's railways is a complex subject whose formative years — those of the 'Railway Mania' and the subsequent formation of a number of small companies that typified the 19th century — are most difficult to cover in short. So many of these early railways were proposed, ratified by Parliament, started, stopped, restarted, stopped again and finally built in a different manner to that originally proposed, that any historian wishing to produce a short appraisal is inevitably and irrevocably caught up in a mesh of intricate and interwoven strands whose description leave the reader unenlightened and confused.

The main difficulty in understanding the growth of the railway network is one of scale: today we accept that one nationalised company manages the whole of Britain's railway network — from 1923 to Nationalisation in 1948 there were four companies. Before 1923, especially in the 1860-1890 period, there were, literally, hundreds of small companies with the desire, but often not the money or expertise, to run a railway. It is difficult to grasp the unplanned and uncoordinated nature of this development and even more difficult to record it in a readable manner although there are many who have tried.

With hindsight it is easy to pick out from the myriad tiny companies the front runners — those whose organisations, leaders and ambitions brought them to the forefront. At the time it was more difficult, just as it was to decide which gauge — broad, 'standard', narrow or even mixed — was to be used. From this splintered hotch-potch of minor concerns and conflicting ideas two companies eventually emerged in the south-west as the railway system began to take on a more unified form — the Great Western Railway and London and South Western Railway. Between them, the numerous lines in Devon and Cornwall became welded into a framework that was to exist, for the most part, until the 1960s. The lines served the major centres of population and industry, providing the main mode of transport for both the local inhabitants and the huge influx of summer visitors that so swelled the season's traffic.

The Grouping of 1923 did not greatly affect the recognised order in Devon and Cornwall except in that the LSWR became part of the Southern Railway. In practice it was indeed the heyday of the steam locomotive and the railways in general, but road competition, especially in the south-west, was beginning to have an effect. During these years the 'Big Four' grouped companies profited from the circumstances to build strong corporate identities. The GWR in particular — 'God's Wonderful Railway' — built up an image that still lingers on in the hearts of enthusiasts.

The old LSWR lines in Southern hands did not fare so well. Dominated by London and its massive commuter belt, the Southern Railway concentrated its energy and money into improving its suburban routes and lines to the south coast by electrification. The company's lines in the

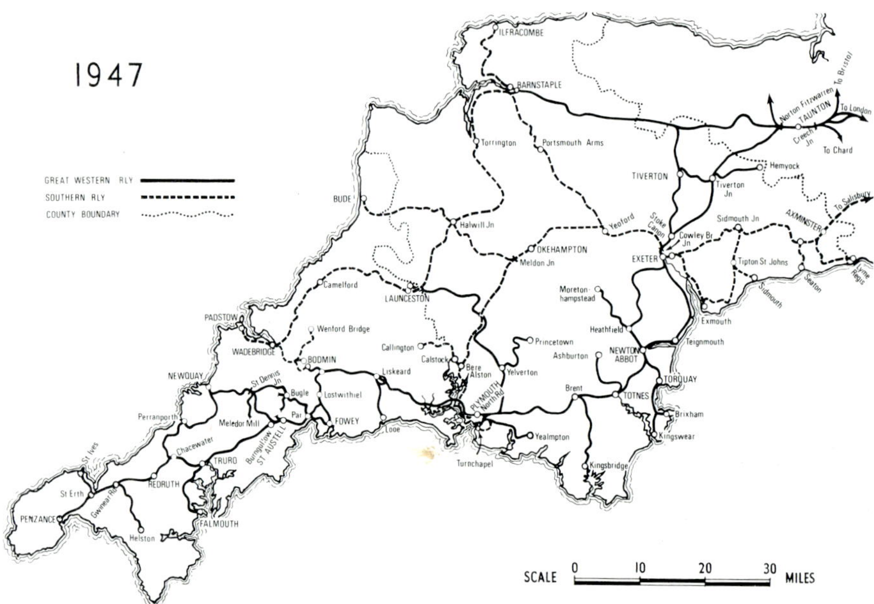

West Country were dubbed by many the Southern's 'withered arm' and, indeed, it was only in postwar years that some of those lines received modern motive power — Bulleid's Light Pacifics — to take the place of the pre-Grouping classes.

The halcyon days of the 1920s gave way to the Depression and the first real sign of how economic problems affected a railway were seen in this period. Uneconomic lines were closed — Bodmin and Wadebridge to Ruthern Bridge and the Lynton and Barnstaple Railway (this a direct result of road competition). It was a foretaste of a problem to come for the railways, and although the later years of the 1930s saw a return to viability, the advent of war sounded a death knell for the Grouped companies.

World War 2 left the railways in an unprecedented condition of disarray and with a six-year backlog of repairs and maintenance. While freight traffic had shown an artificial and temporary increase, passenger traffic had, naturally fallen off. In the west, holiday traffic could not be revived until beach defences were removed, and by the early 1950s the Nationalised system faced competition from the motor car and the 'package' foreign holiday. Attempts to revive this flagging use of the services in postwar years were unsuccessful — typified, perhaps, by the introduction of the Southern's 'Devon Belle' Pullman, with all its 1920s era ambience and even an observation car, on the Waterloo-Ilfracombe route. The 'Devon Belle', an attempt to improve passenger numbers, ran from 1947-54 and then low financial returns led to its termination.

Rising costs, the availability of alternative forms of transport — most obviously the motor car — and the falling passenger figures on the postwar railways led to the need for severe remedial measures. The Nationalisation of Britain's railways in 1948, for better or worse grouped the whole of the system under one body. For Devon and Cornwall this meant little in the operating sense — the Great Western became part of the Western Region of British Railways and the SR part of the Southern Region — but it meant that when steps were taken to make the railways more economic, the surgery was drastic, and affected the whole system.

Today, with hindsight, the cuts that resulted from the Beeching Report might seem inevitable and certainly predestined by earlier actions. At the time the effects were shattering. The eventual closure of so many lines, accompanied as it was by the final transition from steam to diesel and electric traction, not only changed the railway network but also destroyed many of the links with the past. Devon and Cornwall suffered considerably from the 'Beeching Axe' as it became known and a number of branch lines — detailed below — were closed. One can still come across the occasional Great Western or Southern artifact — a station building or a smaller item like a bench or signal, perhaps — but the modern British Rail has produced an identity of its own, divorced to a great extent from the past.

Since the cuts, Devon and Cornwall's railways have remained stable — despite some doubts about the future of some lines, for example the viability of the main line beyond Plymouth. Pared down to its most economic form, the lines are still some of the most photogenic in Britain — from Brunel's bridges to the sea wall at Dawlish. To the modern enthusiast they are still fascinating — especially since the advent of high speed train services from Paddington — but to the older enthusiasts the memories of now defunct lines are still strong. Those lines that were closed in the 1960s are covered in this opening section; later sections cover in more detail the history of existing lines.

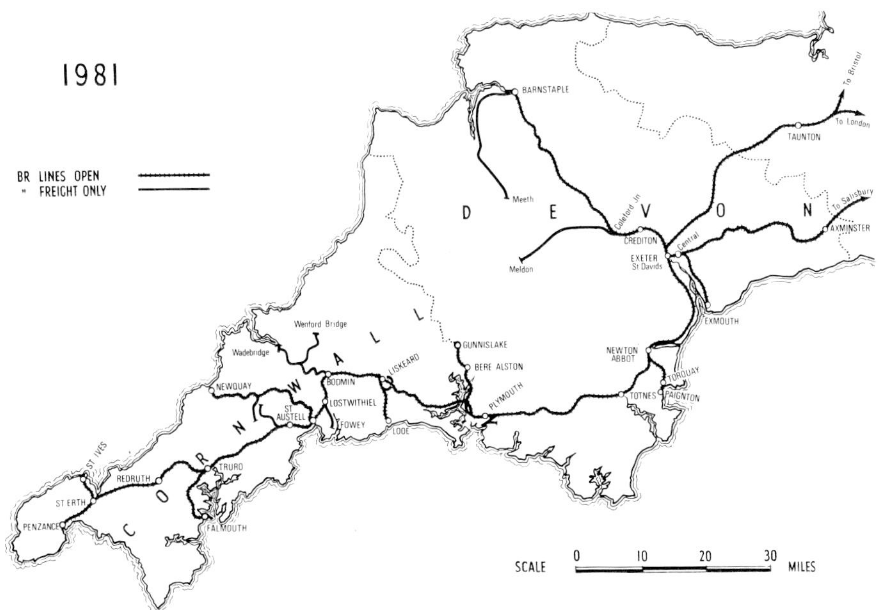

Lyme Regis Branch

Length: 6.75 miles

Proposed in 1845, it was not until 1871 that an agreement was reached between the Lyme Regis Railway Company and the London & South Western Railway for a line from Axminster station on the LSWR main line. However problems in raising capital meant that the project lapsed until 1899 when a Light Railway Order was passed under the 1896 Light Railway Act to enable the Axminster and Lyme Regis Railway to construct the line. After further problems the line finally opened on 24 August 1903 to be worked by the LSWR, who provided £24,000 towards the project.

Because of the light axle-loading restrictions on the line, it was initially operated by two ex-LBSCR 'Terriers' which were succeeded after 1913 by Adams Class 0415 'radial' 4-4-2Ts. In 1928 replacement locomotives were tried on the line, but they failed to keep the schedules due to difficulties on the sharp curves and two of the 4-4-2Ts (which had been laid aside for scrapping) were reinstated. A third, No 30583, was purchased from the East Kent Railway, to whom it had been sold in 1919, and returned to service in 1946.

After Nationalisation, Adams 'radials' soldiered on until the early 1960s when Ivatt Class 2 2-6-2Ts took over. One of the 4-4-2Ts, No 30583, was purchased by the Bluebell Railway and can now be seen at work in Sussex. In November 1963 dmus took over and continued to work the line — with a brief return to steam for periods in 1964/5 because of shortage of dmus — until its closure. Freight traffic over the branch was withdrawn in February 1964 and the passenger workings on 29 November 1965. Like so many other branch lines the Lyme Regis branch was a victim of road competition and was closed following the Beeching Report. The track was lifted in 1967. In 1970 work commenced on a 15in gauge miniature railway using the track bed at Combpyne, but financial difficulties caused abandonment after 1.5 miles had been laid.

Below: Class '0415' 4–4–2T No 30582 is hard at work on the 1 in 40 gradient from Axminster to Combpyne on 7 May 1960. Combpyne, a shelter-less little platform, was the only intermediate station on the branch, and by the 1960s even the holiday traffic to Lyme Regis seldom warranted more than a single coach. *D. Fereday-Glen*

Right: In its final years, like many SR lines in the west, the Lyme Regis branch passed into the jurisdiction of the Western Region. Alterations to the sharper curves enabled LMS-designed Ivatt 2-6-2Ts to work the line and No 41291 is here seen leaving a deserted Combpyne with the 12.10 Axminster-Lyme Regis, formed by a single WR autotrailer, on 10 March 1965. *W. L. Underhay*

Below right: Cannington viaduct was the major civil engineering feature of the Lyme Regis branch. Adams 'Radial' 4–4–2T No 30582 is crossing with the 11.35 Axminster-Lyme Regis on 29 August 1953. *S. C. Nash*

Seaton Branch

Length: 4.25 miles

The Seaton and Beer Railway, authorised on 13 July 1863, ran from a point on the LSWR main line (later known as Seaton Junction) through Colyton and Colyford to Seaton. It was opened, without public celebration, on 16 March 1868 having been leased to the LSWR since 8 March 1867.

The Southern Railway totally rebuilt Seaton station in 1936, the new layout being brought into use on 28 June. The original Italianate structure was replaced by an SR concrete design, typical of the period, the original station canopy being extended at the same time. The engine shed, always a sub-shed of Exmouth Junction (72A), was also rebuilt in concrete at this time and remained in use until 4 November 1963. Its closure, and that of the signalbox on 2 May 1965 resulted from the dieselisation of passenger services and the ending of freight traffic to Seaton.

Right up to 1963 through coaches from Waterloo were included in the summer timetable and indeed the line had flourished during LSWR ownership and under the Southern Railway until Nationalisation. It was proposed for closure in the Beeching Plan, despite some good summer passenger carryings, with some 1,200 passengers on a Saturday in 1964. The lack of winter traffic meant that the line was not viable and, however contentious, the closure took place following transfer to WR control on 7 March 1966. Seaton Junction, which had never been more than a transfer station for the branch, closed on the same date.

It is still possible to travel on part of the branch, between Seaton and Colyton, for on 28 August 1970 the Seaton & District Electric Tramway commenced operation using 2ft 9in gauge replica trams aproximately two-thirds full size.

Below: On a damp 27 January 1962, elderly 'M7' class 0-4-4T No 30667 leaves Seaton for Seaton Junction with a typical three-coach train.

Right: The goods 'lock-up' on the platform end at Colyton is a typical example of SR 1930s modernisation as applied to the branch. The motive power, however, remains somewhat rustic in this August 1959 view of 'M7' 0-4-4T No 30021 heading an evening train for Seaton Junction. *D. Fereday-Glenn*

Below right: A delightful study of ex-LSWR Adams '02' class 0-4-4T No 207 of 1889 standing at Seaton Junction with an autotrain for Seaton. *Real Photos/IA Library*

Sidmouth Branch *Length:* 8.25 miles

Before the advent of the railway there had been several abortive attempts to improve Sidmouth Harbour in a bid to attract trade. An act of 1836 gave permission to enclose an area of 10 acres, using blocks of stone to construct the harbour walls. To convey the stone a 1.5-mile railway, including a 500yd tunnel, was built. A locomotive was acquired and delivered from Exeter but it was found to be too large for the tunnel and was eventually removed in 1838.

At a meeting on 18 December 1861 the Sidmouth Railway and Harbour Company formulated proposals for a railway to Sidmouth together with the construction of a new harbour. The bill received Parliamentary consent in 1862 for the construction of a line from Sidmouth to Feniton on the Salisbury & Yeovil Railway (later LSWR), but the company failed in 1869. A new bill was passed in 1871 and the line eventually opened on 6 July 1874, engineered so that the track could be doubled when traffic demanded. There were stations at Ottery St Mary and Tipton (Tipton St Johns from 1881).

In 1894 the Budleigh Salterton Railway was incorporated and its line from a junction with the Sidmouth Railway at Tipton St Johns to Budleigh Salterton (4.5 miles) opened in May 1897. It was extended to Exmouth (total 11.5 miles) in June 1903.

The Sidmouth Railway remained nominally independent until 1922 when its shares were exchanged for LSWR shares and that railway became part of the new Southern Railway in 1923. The Regional boundary changes of 1 January 1963 transferred the line to the Western Region of BR and closure proposals in the Beeching Report of the same year were resisted by local organisations. Dieselisation and rationalisation of facilities followed, with the withdrawal of through coaches at the end of summer 1965. Passengers for London then deserted the branch and travelled by road to Axminster.

The availability of a replacement bus service facilitated closure on 6 March 1967 and the Budleigh Salterton line closed at the same time. Tipton St Johns had been the last junction between two single lines in the West Country and at the of closure was still handling 30 trains a day. The connection at Sidmouth Junction was taken out when the main line was singled but Sidmouth Junction station was reopened as Feniton in May 1971.

Below: Class 'M7' 0-4-4T No 30044 drifts down from Budleigh Salterton towards the junction at Tipton St Johns with an early morning local from Exmouth on 13 April 1955. *David J. Beaver*

Right: A scene at Tipton St Johns on 11 March 1961. The 12.58 Sidmouth Junction-Sidmouth/Exmouth has just divided and the first two coaches have gone forward to Sidmouth. Watched by the shunter, 'M7' 0-4-4-T No 30024 backs down on to the Exmouth portion. *J. C. Haydon*

Below right: On 15 August 1964 a two-car dmu forming the 12.15 from Sidmouth Junction arrives at Sidmouth, as BR Standard 2-6-4T No 80038 and 2-6-2T No 82035 wait with the ecs of the 08.03 (SO) through train from Waterloo *I. G. Holt*

Hemyock Branch

Length: 7.5 miles

Powers for construction of the Culm Valley line were obtained in 1873 under the little-used Regulation of Railways Act 1868 and it completed the railway map in the Tiverton area. Local landowners and farmers subscribed to the cheap construction of the line and large profits were envisaged from the little line which served the villages of Uffculme and Culmstock on its 7.5-mile route from Tiverton Junction to Hemyock. However, construction costs were almost double the estimate, the work took two years longer than anticipated and receipts were barely half the estimate. The line opened on 29 May 1876 and by 1880 the shareholders were so disillusioned that they disposed of the line to the Great Western Railway for £33,000.

The GWR fared better when a textile mill was opened, and in the 20th century milk traffic from the dairy at Hemyock increased dramatically. Passenger traffic from the tiny stations was very limited and the 1959 timetable shows just three down and four up trains, the fastest of these taking 38 minutes for the 7.5 miles (less than 15mph)! The branch was restricted to use by the lightest locomotives and latterly these were '14xx' class 0-4-2Ts. A single gas-lit brake second coach was used, as the low speed was insufficient to charge the batteries of an electrically lit vehicle and in any case longer, more modern vehicles could not work round the sharp curves. Passenger services succumbed to closure on 9 September 1963 but the line remained open for traffic from the creamery until the early 1970s, being worked by the North British-built Class 22 diesel-hydraulics.

Below: The Hemyock branch was one of Devon's best-loved rural byways. On 22 June 1963 '14xx' 0-4–2T No 1450 (now preserved on the Dart Valley Railway) heads the 09.20 (SO) Tiverton Junction-Hemyock away from the delightful Culmstock station. *G. D. King*

Right: Milk traffic was always more lucrative than passengers on the Hemyock branch, as amply demonstrated by this vew of '14xx' 0-4–2T No 1462 waiting at the terminus with a mixed train for Tiverton Junction on 24 February 1962. *T. W. Nicolls*

Below right: In the final years of the branch, NBL Class 22 B-B No D6330 creeps away from the main line at Tiverton Junction with the 13.45 Exeter-Hemyock milk empties on 15 July 1970. Not only has the branch now gone, but the diesel-hydraulics are no more, and all West Country milk now travels by road. *John M. Boyes*

Exe Valley Line and Tiverton Branch

Length: Exe Valley 21.25 miles
Tiverton Branch 4.75 miles

Tiverton was first reached by rail on 12 June 1848 with the opening of the short branch to the Bristol & Exeter Railway (B&ER) at Tiverton Junction. It was a broad gauge line built by the B&ER with no intermediate stations but two passing loops. An intermediate halt was later built at Halberton by the GWR. The line was converted to standard gauge in 1884 in order to connect with the Exe Valley line which was standard gauge from the outset.

Authorised in 1874 and opened on 1 May 1885 the Exe Valley Railway connected Tiverton to the B&ER main line at Stoke Canon, three miles north of Exeter. The line was extended northwards by the Exe Valley North Railway and joined the Taunton-Barnstaple line at Morebath, services terminating at an island platform at Dulverton.

The line retained an adequate passenger service to the end, with nine trains each day on weekdays, a reduced Saturday service and no Sunday trains. There was a single freight train in each direction on weekdays. The route followed the River Exe closely and was extremely picturesque. Latterly, most services were worked by '14xx' 0-4-2Ts with one or more auto-trailers but in its final years NBL Class 22 diesels sometimes appeared.

Passenger services on the Exe Valley line ceased on 7 October 1963 although the section between Stoke Canon and Thorverton survived for freight until 30 November 1966. The branch from Tiverton Junction to Tiverton closed to passengers on 5 October 1964, the section onwards from Tiverton to West Exe being used for storage of condemned wagons at this time.

In 1965 Lord Amery purchased '14xx' 0-4-2T No 1442 which had regularly worked the Tiverton branch services which were nicknamed locally the 'Tivvy Bumper' and presented it to the town. Initially it was displayed on a plinth but has since been moved indoors to form the centrepiece of Tiverton Museum's railway section.

Below: The scenic delights of the Exe Valley line are evident in this view of '14xx' 0-4-2T No 1466 (now preserved at Didcot Railway Centre) heading a Dulverton-Exeter autotrain near Bampton on 8 June 1961. *M. J. Fox*

Right: Typical of Exe Valley line architecture was the station at Cadeleigh which is now a private house. The line was specially equipped for maintenance by platelayers using motorised trolleys such as the one shown here, being provided with a 'ganger's key' which when inserted into lineside telephone apparatus enabled the single line token instruments at either end of the section to be locked. Gangers could thus obtain possession of the line without making long journeys to collect or return the token. *J. H. Russell*

Below right: The 'Tivvy Bumper' formed by '14xx' 0-4-2T No 1450 and a 1951-built autotrailer waits at Tiverton on 26 September 1964 before working back to the main line Tiverton Junction station. *M. J. Fox*

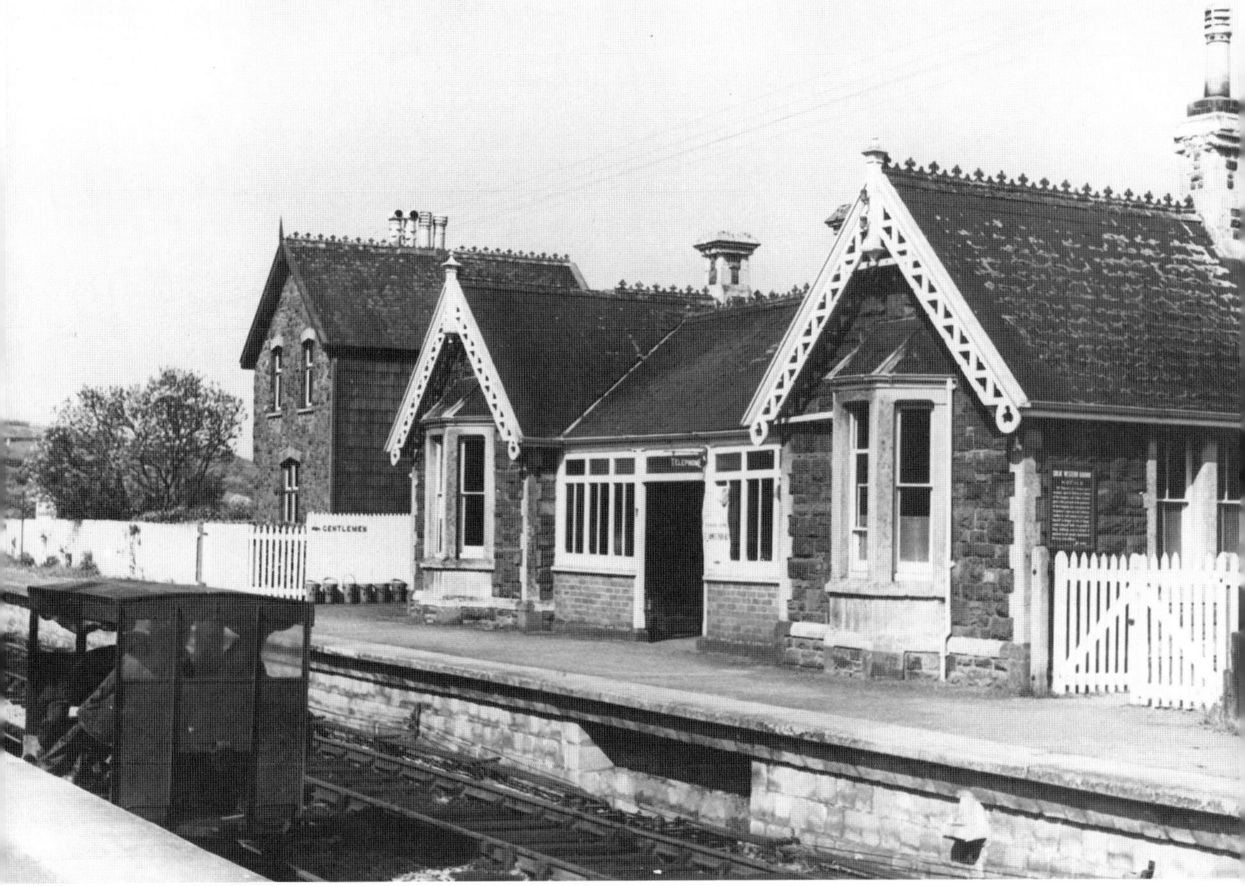
GENTLEMEN
TELEPHONE

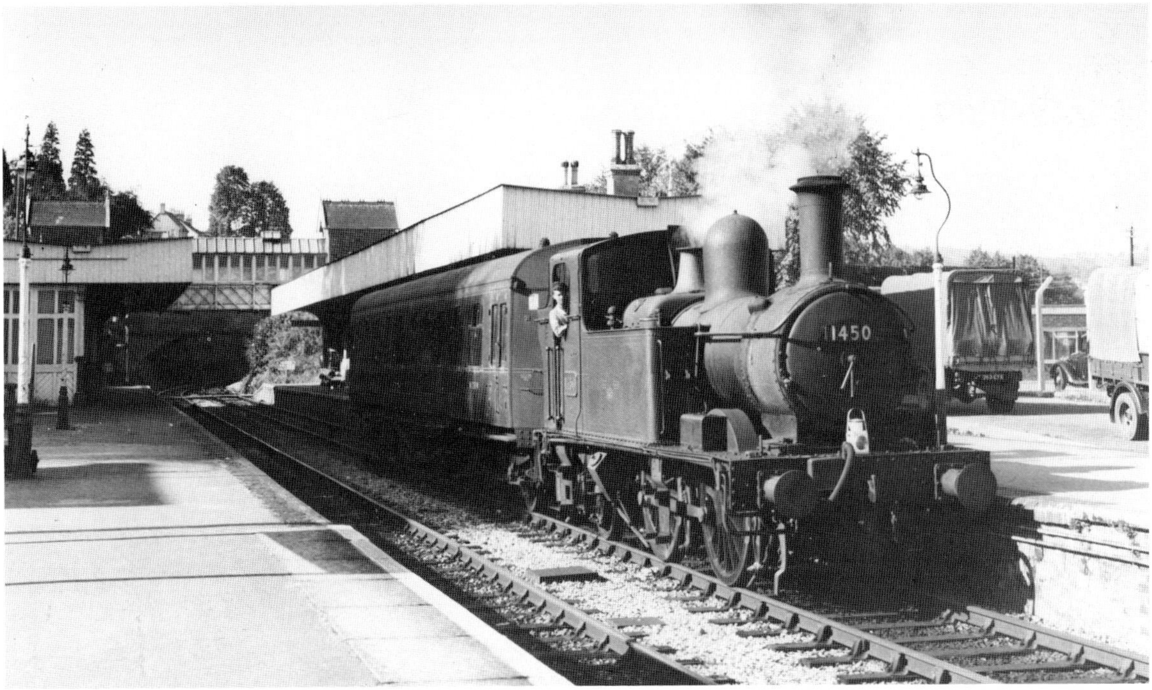
1450

Moretonhampstead Branch and the Teign Valley Line

Length: Moretonhampstead Branch 12.25 miles Teign Valley Line 16 miles

The Moretonhampstead and South Devon Railway was incorporated in 1862 and, as the name suggests, it was to be worked by the South Devon Railway although they only subscribed £500 of the £105,000 capital. The line was built to broad gauge, commencing at Newton Abbot and climbing 550ft to its terminus on Dartmoor. Between Teigngrace and Bovey Tracey, the largest intermediate station, it followed the route of the Haytor Tramway. There were other intermediate stations at Heathfield and at the picture-postcard village of Lustleigh, where the tourist-conscious station master kept a visitors' book. Despite its long climb on to the moors, the line possessed no major engineering works. From 1906 the GWR operated motor buses between Chagford and Moretonhampstead to connect with trains.

Traffic proved quite encouraging until World War 1 but thereafter the service was poor and no attempt was made to win back traffic. As a result the branch failed to survive even until the Beeching Report, and closed on 2 March 1959. A recommendation that this might be reconsidered when diesel units became available was quietly forgotten although the track between Bovey and the terminus was retained until 1971. South of Bovey the line remained in use for traffic to a malting plant, but was later cut back and now reaches as far as Heathfield to serve a banana ripening plant and an oil depot. The station at Moretonhampstead was a perfect example of the small Brunel-designed train shed with stone offices and a timber roof, while the signalbox was an unusual lean-to structure attached to the small locomotive shed.

Although many attempts were made to bypass the coastal Exeter-Newton Abbot section of the GWR, the Teign Valley line required no less than nine Acts of Parliament and two promoting companies before it was eventually built. It diverged from the main line at City Basin Junction, Exeter, and served the villages of Ide, Christow, Ashton, Trusham and Chudleigh before joining the Moretonhampstead branch at Heathfield. It opened between Heathfield and Ashton on 9 October 1882 as an isolated section of standard gauge until the Moretonhampstead branch was converted. The section onwards to Exeter, with two tunnels and numerous cuttings, did not open until 1 July 1902, the complete route being known by the GWR as the Teign Valley line.

Although it was useful as a diversionary route, it generated little traffic of its own, the Exeter-Christow section being closed completely from 9 June 1958. The rest of the line remained open for freight to Trusham concrete works until damaged by flooding in September 1960.

Below: The pretty little station at Bovey Tracey, seen on 28 February 1959, just a few days before closure. *M. Windeatt*

Right: The Brunel-type broad gauge station building at Moretonhampstead looking towards Newton Abbot with '14xx' 0-4-2T No 1466 having just arrived. *M. Windeatt*

Below right: The photographer has caught the eye of driver and passenger on the Newton Abbot-Moretonhampstead autotrain seen here near Heathfield in the late 1940s. *M. M. South*

Plymouth-Launceston Line and Princetown Branch

The Plymouth & Dartmoor Railway was opened in 1823 as a horse-worked tramway between Plymouth and granite quarries at King Tor on Dartmoor. It was built to the so-called 'Dartmoor gauge' of 4ft 6in. Its northern section was taken over by the Princetown Railway which opened its standard gauge branch from Yelverton-Princetown in 1883. Rival schemes were proposed by the LSWR and the South Devon Railway (SDR) to link Plymouth and Tavistock in 1846 but neither line was built. Eventually after protracted wrangling the South Devon & Tavistock Railway began work on its line on 24 September 1856. There were three tunnels and six timber viaducts carried on stone piers. The largest of these was the last to be rebuilt in brick, during 1910. The line opened for passengers on 22 June 1859 and for freight on 1 February 1860 and was leased to the SDR who purchased it in 1865. It was a broad gauge line with stations at Marsh Mills, Bickleigh and Horrabridge.

Two independent schemes placed before Parliament in 1861 led the SDR to protect its interests by proposing extension of the line to Launceston. The proposal was passed with the proviso that the Board of Trade be empowered to order the laying of mixed gauge track when required. It was opened to passengers on 1 July 1865 and, like the earlier section, was worked by the SDR until absorbed by them in 1873.

During World War 2 connection to the adjacent SR station was installed at Launceston for military traffic and this opened on 22 September 1943. Traffic was then concentrated on the SR station and the GWR station, known as Launceston North, was closed on 30 June 1952. Both Launceston and Tavistock were also served by SR routes and the GWR line served no other large towns, so it is hardly surprising that it closed on 31 December 1962. Services on the SR lines outlasted it by only a few years.

The Princetown branch was probably the most desolate and remote piece of railway in the West Country. Originally it joined the Tavistock line at Horrabridge, in a northerly direction but in 1885 a new junction station was provided at Yelverton and the branch was altered to make a southerly facing connection. The branch climbed from 500ft at Yelverton to its terminus 1,400ft above sea level, in a series of twists and turns around the hills which provided breathtaking views.

There were no passing places on the single track and speed was limited to 20mph throughout. There were a few halting places, however, and their names paint a poetic image of Dartmoor — Dousland, Prowse's Crossing, Burrator Platform, Lowry Road Crossing, Ingra Tor, Swell Tor Siding and King Tor.

Princetown with its infamous Dartmoor Prison was a forbidding place, and its severe-looking stone-built station was very much in keeping with the rugged desolate surroundings. The passenger service, maintained by the small-wheeled '44xx' class 2-6-2Ts was withdrawn on 5 March 1956.

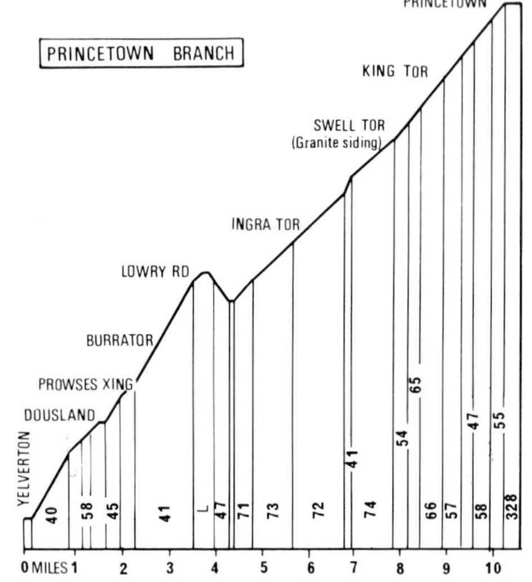

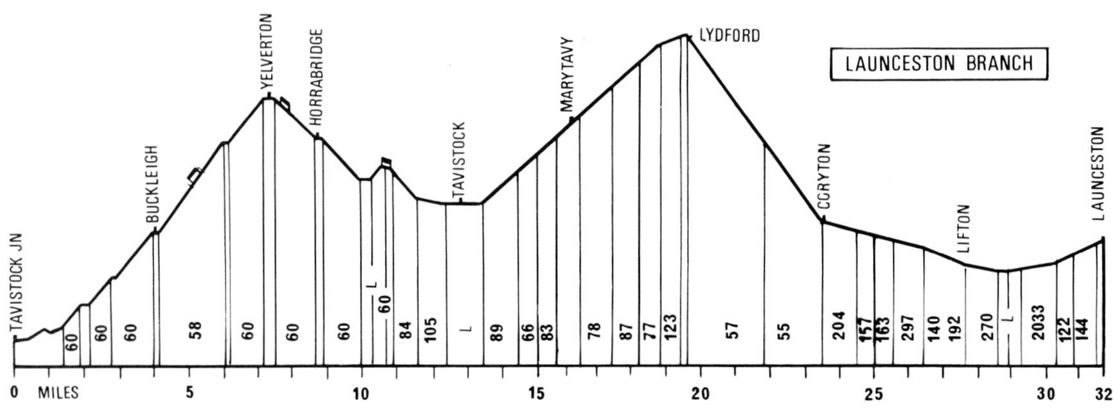

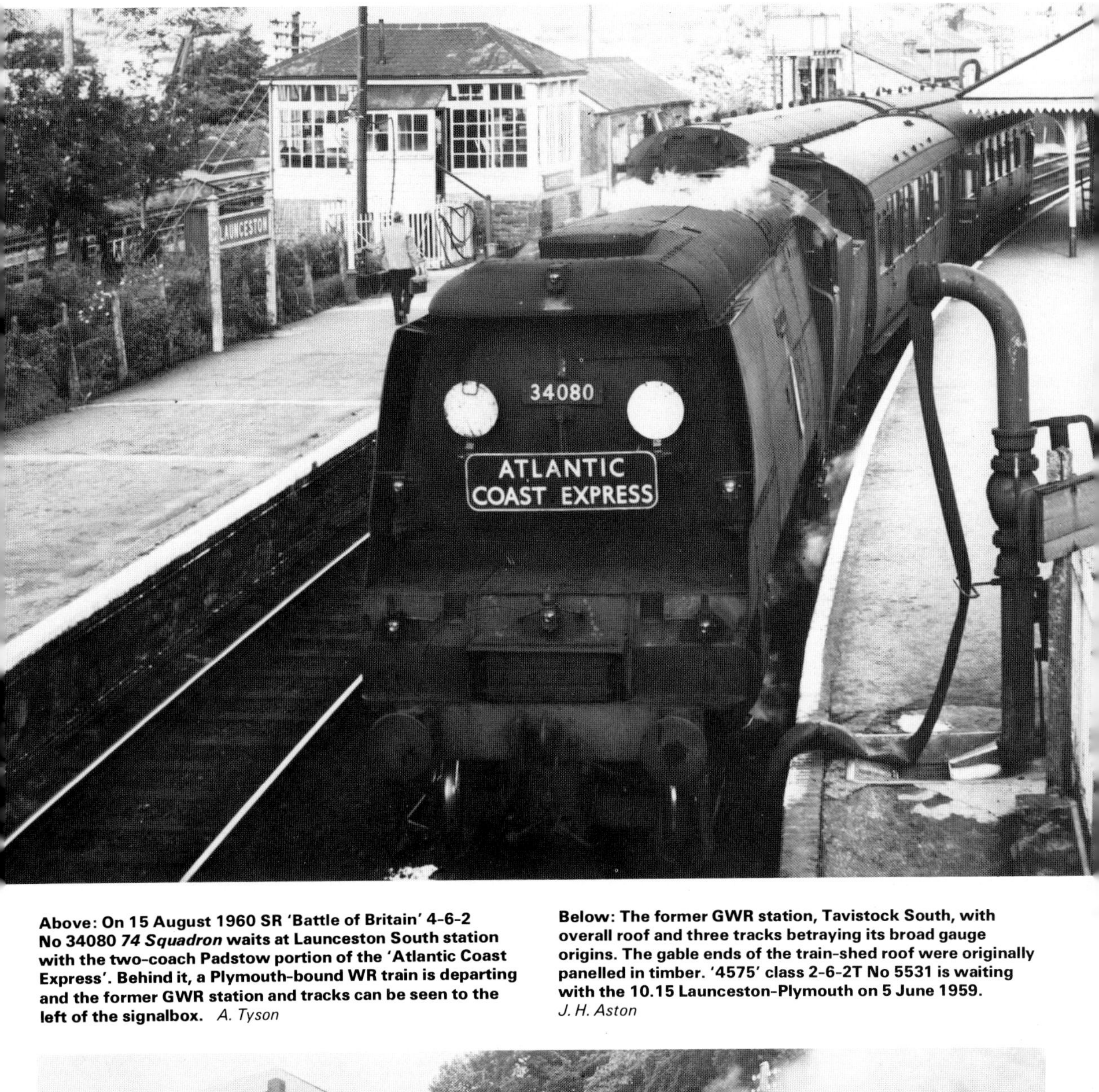

Above: On 15 August 1960 SR 'Battle of Britain' 4-6-2 No 34080 *74 Squadron* waits at Launceston South station with the two-coach Padstow portion of the 'Atlantic Coast Express'. Behind it, a Plymouth-bound WR train is departing and the former GWR station and tracks can be seen to the left of the signalbox.   *A. Tyson*

Below: The former GWR station, Tavistock South, with overall roof and three tracks betraying its broad gauge origins. The gable ends of the train-shed roof were originally panelled in timber. '4575' class 2-6-2T No 5531 is waiting with the 10.15 Launceston-Plymouth on 5 June 1959.
J. H. Aston

Above: The highest station on the Great Western Railway was Princetown, 1,373ft above sea level, seen here on 17 April 1954 with a Caravan Club special train, unusually heavy for the branch, departing behind '44xx' 2-6-2T No 4410. *B. A. Butt*

Below: Remnants of the Dartmoor Railway at King Tor quarry in 1953. *M. E. Ware*

Yealmpton Branch *Length:* 6.5 miles

The branch to Yealmpton was a curious outpost of the Great Western Railway and opened to passenger traffic on 17 January 1898 and to freight a day later. It was divorced from the rest of the GWR system and made physical connection with the LSWR at Plymstock. There were intermediate stations at Billacombe, Elburton Cross, Steer Point and Brixton Road and the branch was single track and worked by electric train staff.

Being entirely within the Plymouth urban area, the line was soon in unequal competition with other forms transport and was closed to passengers on 7 July 1930. It remained in use for freight, the 1939 working timetable showing one train in each direction on weekdays only.

Passenger services were reinstated on 3 November 1941 in connection with wartime arrangements, but operated to and from Plymouth Friary (SR) station. The line closed again on 6 October 1947 but although the track has been lifted, some buildings remain intact in private use. The SR line to Plymstock remains in use for cement traffic.

Below: The Yealmpton branch autotrain approaches the terminus, headed by '54xx' 0-6-0PT No 5412 in September 1946. *B. A. Butt*

Kingswear and Brixham Branches

Length: Kingswear-Paignton 6.75 miles
Churston-Brixham 2 miles

When ships based at Dartmouth commenced a feeder service up the River Dart to Totnes station it had an adverse effect on traffic on the short Torquay branch. The Dartmouth and Torbay Railway (D&TR) was incorporated in 1857 to extend the Torquay branch and the first section to Paignton opened on 2 August 1859. This short length contained some 20 bridges, a viaduct and a tunnel, the latter being opened out in 1910. The next three miles to Brixham Road (later called Churston) opened on 14 March 1861.

A change of plan then caused delays, as the D&TR proposed to cross the River Dart and enter Dartmouth with a line on the west bank of the river. However, this plan was defeated in the House of Lords due to opposition by the landowner concerned. Instead, the 3.75 miles from Churston to Kingswear eventually opened on 16 August 1864, together with the ferry service across the river to Dartmouth.

The Torbay and Brixham Railway opened on 28 February 1868 as a result of the efforts of one man, R. W. Wolston. In a bid to help trade in the little fishing port he subscribed to 1,770 of the 1,800 £10 shares and went on to complete the line when the contractor failed.

He allowed the South Devon Railway to work the line as his agents but was twice forced into litigation in order to obtain a fair return on his investment. The line was eventually sold to the Great Western in 1883 for £12,000.

Brixham station was inconveniently sited high above the town and the service was simply a shuttle to Churston where a change of train was necessary for onward travel. Although there was a good traffic in fish, the line was unable to sustain its passenger service, and closed on 13 May 1963. Following rationalisation the Paignton-Kingswear section survived as a dmu shuttle service until October 1972 when it was transferred to the Torbay Steam Railway section of the Dart Valley Railway.

Below: On 23 June 1952 '14xx' 0-4-2T No 1466 waits at Brixham with the autotrain for Churston. *W. S. Garth*

Right: On 25 August 1952 No 1466 was still working the Brixham branch, and it is here seen running into Churston. *R. J. Buckley*

Below right: The railway follows the shore line of the Dart estuary at Kingswear. On 26 August 1954 No 7812 *Erlestoke Manor* makes a rousing start from the terminus with the 15.25 to Newton Abbot. *R. K. Evans*

Kingsbridge Branch

Length: 12.5 miles

The railway came to Kingsbridge in the last century and initially the popular harbour town was served by road coaches from the SDR main line at Wrangaton, known at that time as Kingsbridge Road. A branch railway to Kingsbridge was commenced in 1860 but later abandoned for want of capital. The line ran from Brent, which had been a passing point on the single track SDR main line, until the track was later doubled. With the eventual opening of the branch on 19 December 1893, Brent station was rebuilt in standard GWR style.

The branch was provided with small stone-built intermediate stations at Avonwick, Gara Bridge and Loddiswell, that at Gara Bridge having a passing loop and a level crossing. The Kingsbridge terminus was extensive but was scarcely justified, save for the influx of tourist traffic during the summer. It was closed on 16 September 1963 not long after single-unit diesel railcars had taken over the service. The stations at Avonwick and Gara Bridge are now private dwellings, the former being let as a holiday home.

Below: A Gloucester RCW single-unit railcar approaches the tunnel at the summit of the climb from Kingsbridge on 12 August 1961. *R. E. Toop*

Right: Kingsbridge basks in the sun on 18 September 1957 as '4575' 2-6-2T No 5533 waits with the 16.15 to Brent *J. D. Wood*

Below right: The prototype Gloucester RCW single unit railcar No W55000 clatters away from Dainton tunnel on 23 September 1961, working the 16.28 Newton Abbot-Kingsbridge. *W. L. Underhay*

KINGSBRIDGE
C2

Taunton-Barnstaple Line
Length: 43.75 miles

The first plans to link Taunton and Barnstaple by rail were mooted in the 1840s but the Act enabling construction of the line was not passed until July 1864. Work commenced in 1865 and in the the same year agreement was reached for the Bristol & Exeter Railway (B&ER) to work the line. The first section from the main line at Norton Fitzwarren to Wivelscombe opened to traffic on 8 June 1871 and then financial difficulties led the company to lay off all its navvies. It was finally opened through to the terminus at Barnstaple Victoria Road in November 1873. Throughout its existence the company was in dire financial straits and it was eventually absorbed by the GWR in 1901.

The line was built to broad gauge and was converted to standard in 1881. A connection to the LSWR Barnstaple Junction station was opened on 1 June 1887 but trains continued to call at Victoria Road, necessitating a reversal for which five minutes was allowed in the timetable. In June 1960 a new connection was provided, enabling Victoria Road to be closed and all trains then ran direct to the junction station. In 1876 the B&ER increased the number of passing loops and made improvements at Barnstaple to simplify operation. During the 1930s the GWR double-tracked the section between Norton Fitzwarren and Milverton and, unusual for a GWR line, automatic tablet-catcher apparatus was installed.

There were intermediate stations at Norton Fitzwarren, Milverton, Wiveliscombe, Venn Cross, Morebath, Morebath Junction halt, Dulverton, East Anstey, Yeo Mill halt, Bishops Nympton & Molland, Filleigh and Swimbridge. The major engineering features were the lattice-girder Tone Viaduct and Venn Cross tunnel, both on the section between Venn Cross and Wiveliscombe.

Freight services over the line were withdrawn in August 1964 and despite dieselisation and some economies the passenger service was withdrawn, after a short reprieve, on 30 October 1966. The line offered some of the most splendid scenery available by rail in Devon and the very last train was an inspection special for BR officials. Many of the station buildings are now private dwellings.

Above: The 12.20 through train from Ilfracombe-Barnstaple leaving Dulverton, behind '53xx' 2-6-0 No 5336 on 22 August 1964. Such workings sometimes brought SR Moguls to the line. At left the remains of the yard and the Exe Valley line bay platform are being removed. *M. J. Fox*

Left: One of the ubiquitous '43xx' 2-6-0s crosses the Tone Viaduct between Venn Cross and Wiveliscombe. *Gainsborough*

Above right: Taunton-Barnstaple services were dieselised some two years before closure. Here the 10.40 from Barnstaple is seen just after leaving Milverton on the double track section to Norton Fitzwarren on 21 September 1965. *H.A. Dunn*

Right: Barnstaple Junction station on 30 April 1964 with SR Light Pacific No 34015 *Exmouth* and 'N' class 2-6-0 No 31840 in the ramshackle SR shed as WR '43xx' 2-6-0 No 7303 departs with the 14.24 to Taunton. *M. York*

Lynton & Barnstaple Railway

The most charismatic of the West Country railways, and also the most tragic loss, was the Lynton & Barnstaple Railway (L&BR). The L&BR Bill received Royal Assent on 27 June 1895. It was largely the result of the efforts of Sir George Newnes, publisher, who lived at Lynton and was responsible for building the cliff lift between the twin villages of Lynton and Lynmouth. Work on the L&BR commenced on 17 September 1895 but grave difficulties were encountered as the contractor underestimated the nature of the land and therefore the cost of construction. Expensive litigation followed, and although the L&BR won through in the end, it was left financially crippled even before the first train ran. It was built to the narrow (1ft 11in) gauge in order to simplify construction and make minimum impact on the splendid scenery through which it ran.

The line opened amid much ceremony on 11 May 1898. There were small intermediate stations at Chelfham and Bratton Fleming, and larger ones at Blackmoor Gate and Woody Bay. The Lynton terminus was badly sited high above the village in an effort to make it inconspicuous — a tragic mistake which badly affected potential traffic. At Barnstaple Town station, a new joint station with the LSWR, there was a cross-platform interchange to trains for Ilfracombe or Waterloo. Halts were later built at Snapper, Parracombe and Caffyns Down. The L&BR purchased three Manning Wardle 2-6-2Ts named *Yeo*, *Exe* and *Taw*, modern bogie carriages including some observation cars, and a selection of freight stock for the opening. Later it acquired a fourth locomotive, the American Baldwin-built 2-4-2T *Lyn*. The line's best years

were prior to World War 1 and following negotiations for takeover by the LSWR, it became part of the Southern Railway at the Grouping of 1923.

The SR tended to apply main-line standards to what the locals considered their 'toy railway' and in due course another 2-6-2T named *Lew* and further goods wagons were purchased desptie the fact that the old L&BR had not needed further equipment. It never proved possible to get the journey time down below 1.5 hours for the 20 miles and, meanwhile, road improvements were giving advantages to the bus and the motor car.

By the mid-1930s the SR was deeply committed to its suburban electrification programme and there was little sympathy for the loss-making narrow gauge anachronism in North Devon. When track renewals became necessary the SR posted closure notices for the line. Local people organised a protest meeting, but when they all turned up by car, there was little more that could be said. So the Lynton & Barnstaple closed on 29 September 1935 and its equipment was auctioned on 13 November. Almost all the pretty little locomotives and rolling stock were reduced to scrap at Barnstaple.

It is still possible to trace most of the route, and all the stations survive as private dwellings, some of them available for rent as holiday homes. The station at Blackmoor Gate is now a licensed restaurant and the locomotive shed and workshops at Barnstaple house local industries. There has recently been a move to rebuild part of the line as a preserved railway, but with little of the original equipment surviving it will be scarcely possible to recreate the magic of the old L&BR.

Below left: The American-built Baldwin 2-4-2T *Lyn* as SR No 762 outside the shed at Pilton, Barnstaple in the early 1930s. *Real Photos*

Above: An early 1930s scene at Barnstaple Town station, with 2-6-2T No 188 *Lew* waiting with a short train for Lynton. *Real Photos*

Below: A very early view of Lynton station with an up train waiting to depart behind one of the 2-6-2Ts which has had its polish worked in the distinctive 'fish-tail' pattern. *Ian Allan Library*

Ilfracombe Branch *Length:* 15 miles

A high ridge of ground immediately behind the town made rail access to the popular resort of Ilfracombe extremely difficult. Nevertheless, there were numerous schemes proposed for providing railways, including rival proposals by the LSWR and Devon and Somerset Railways in 1864. Eventually there was an agreement for a mixed gauge line but this did not proceed and a new LSWR scheme received Royal Assent on 4 July 1870. Although the Devon and Somerset operated a rival road service, the line eventually opened on 20 July 1874.

It contained considerable heavy engineering works, notably the Mortehoe bank ($2\frac{1}{4}$ miles at 1 in 36) and terminated in a substantial station high above Ilfracombe. There were intermediate stations at Mortehoe & Woolacombe and Braunton. Later a new station was opened at Barnstaple Town to connect with the Lynton & Barnstaple Railway, and during World War 2 a station was opened to serve the Air Force station near Barnstaple and appropriately named Wrafton. The long curved iron bridge over the Taw estuary at Barnstaple was a local landmark, while at the other end of the line the views to seaward on the approach to Ilfracombe were spectacular. The line was doubled in stages between 1889-91 with the exception of the Taw bridge. On 1 July 1905 the opening of the east spur at Barnstaple Victoria Road enabled through running via the GWR to Taunton. The spur was closed in 1939 and trains were then obliged to reverse at Victoria Road until it was reinstated on 13 June 1960.

The Ilfracombe branch became well known when it provided the nickname for the Beattie 'Ilfracombe Goods' 0-6-0 design of 1874. It received much attention in the early 1950s when the 'Devon Belle' Pullman train was introduced between Waterloo-Ilfracombe, providing a luxury all-Pullman service complete with observation car. The latter was turned on the turntable at Ilfracombe in the evening after each journey. This attempt to win back traffic was really misguided and years too late since a luxury 1930s-style service was scarely an answer to rising competition from cheap motor car touring and package continental holidays. The service only lasted a few years.

The Ilfracombe branch passed into WR control in 1963 and the service was dieselised and the line later singled as traffic declined. It was eventually closed on 5 October 1970 in spite of local opposition. A controversial scheme to reopen the line under private ownership failed and was the subject of a Board of Trade investigation. Braunton signalbox has been acquired for preservation and here and at Mortehoe the derelict stations still stand. Ilfracombe station site has been completely redeveloped with factory premises.

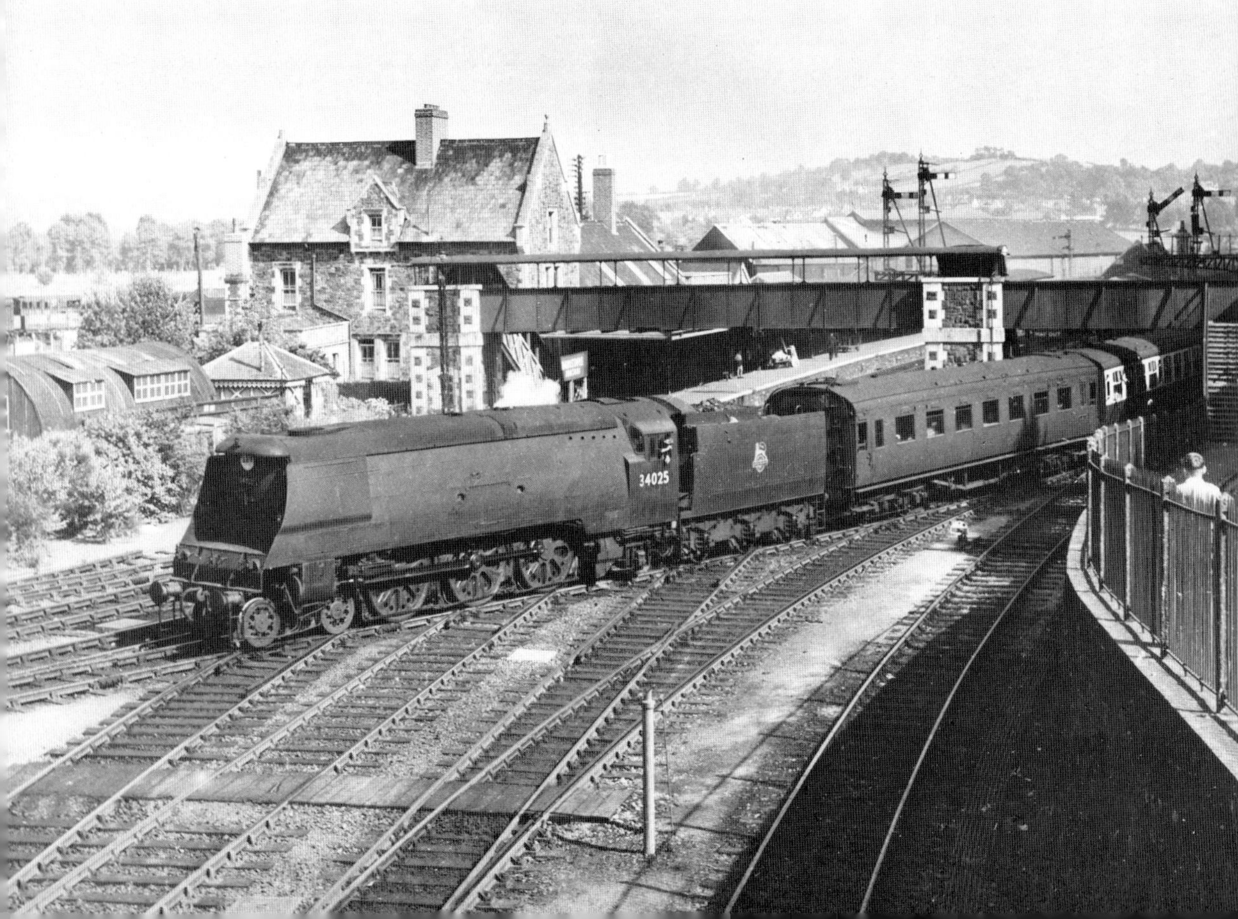

Left: The only survivor of Barnstaple's three stations is Barnstaple Junction, sadly reduced in status since this photograph was taken on 11 August 1955. SR Light Pacific No 34025 *Whimple* is making its way over the complex junction towards the Taw bridge with through coaches from Waterloo. *R. E. Vincent*

Above: On the last day of passenger services a Class 117 dmu forms the 08.10 Ilfracombe-Exeter St Davids seen here crossing the Taw estuary at high tide after calling at Barnstaple Town station. *M. J. Squire*

Centre right: Braunton stands derelict and vandalised awaiting the bulldozers — a sad end, but typical of many West Country stations.

Bottom right: By contrast a scene filled with the hope of a prosperous future as carpenters complete the roof of Ilfracombe station in 1874. *E. J. C. Daniell*

Bideford, Westward Ho! and Appledore Railway — *Length:* 7 miles

The Bideford, Westward Ho! and Appledore Railway (BWH&AR) was one of those railway oddities born out of local desire to have a railway service, no matter how absurd. After early, grandiose schemes to link Appledore to the LSWR failed due to the town's difficult position on the end of a peninsula, the BWH&AR built its seven-mile line in total isolation. It ran as a street-tramway through Bideford from the Quay to Westward Ho! and Northam and was opened on 24 April 1901. By this time it had become a subsidiary of the huge British Electric Traction group and thus doubly peculiar in being operated by steam. The extension to Appledore opened as a conventional light railway on 1 May 1908.

Intermediate stops were provided at Chanters Lane, The Causeway, Kenwith Castle, Mudcott, Abbotsham Road, Cornborough Cliffs, Westward Ho!, Beach Road, Northam and Richmond Road. The services were worked by three Hunslet 2-4-2Ts (Nos 713/4/5) named *Grenville*, *Kinsley* and *Torridge* which were equipped with side-skirting down almost to rail level for street operation. There were just two third class carriages of American-style design with end platforms and steps to ground level. They were unique among standard-gauge vehicles in having a centre buffer-coupling.

The little railway spent its short life in abject poverty despite such curious marketing stunts as the hire of blacked up 'Minstrels' to play at the stations. It also provided detailed charges for the conveyance of diverse merchandise such as 'a bitch or litter of puppies in a hamper for 1s 0d, or a harp (in or out of case) for 2s 0d'.

The exact details of its closure are lost in the mists of obscurity but apparently all its equipment was requisitioned by the Government in 1917. Services ceased on 28 March that year, and the locomotives were run over temporary track on Bideford road bridge to reach the LSWR line. Various reports suggest that the locomotives subsequently appeared in France, or were lost at sea off the Cornish Coast. However, one is known to have been sold by the Ministry of Munitions to the National Smelting Co, being finally scrapped in 1937. One of the coaches was cut in half to serve as beach huts at Westward Ho!

Left: BW&AR 2-4-0T *Grenville* **stands at Bideford Quay with one of the distinctive open balcony coaches.**
L&GRP (Neg 25038)

Torrington & Marland Light Railway — *Length:* 5.5 miles

The Torrington & Marland Light Railway was an industrial freight line built by the Marland North Devon Clay Company to transport china clay to Torrington. Before the railway, clay had been sent by road to Torrington and then by barge down the River Torridge to Bideford. It was opened in 1880 as a 3ft gauge line using three Fletcher Jennings 0-4-0STs originally supplied for construction of the breakwater at St Helier, Jersey. They were found to be too heavy for the 30lb rail of the Marland system and were rebuilt as 'tender' locomotives by placing the water tanks on a separate wagon. There were a number of other locomotives including two long wheelbase 0-6-0s specially designed for weight distribution on the rickety Torrington viaduct.

At its Torrington end the line was taken over by the North Devon and Cornwall Junction Railway and converted to standard gauge as part of the Halwill Junction-Torrington line which opened in 1925. Production of china clay continues at Meeth.

Top right: The Marland Railway's rickety timber viaduct over the River Torridge at Torrington. It was rebuilt to form part of the Torrington-Halwill Junction line. *Ian Allan Library*

Bottom right: An unidentified 0-6-0T at the North Devon Clay Company's Peters Marland works. Note the kettle on the smokebox beside the chimney! *LPC/Ian Allan Library*

Barnstaple-Halwill Junction   *Length:* 34.75 miles

The first section of this route, between Barnstaple Junction and Fremington, was built by the Taw Valley Railway & Docks Company and opened in August 1854. Powers for the extension to Bideford were transferred from this company to the Bideford Extension Company by Act of Parliament in 1853 and the extension was amalgamated with the LSWR from 1 January 1865. In the same year the LSWR was authorised to extend southwards to Torrington to connect with the proposed Devon & Cornwall line. The latter was not built and it was well into the 20th century before the rails extended beyond Torrington.

Eventually, thanks to the efforts of that prodigious light railway builder, Col H. F. Stephens, the North Devon & Cornwall Junction Railway was authorised to build a line from Torrington to Halwill Junction. The first sod was cut on 30 June 1922 and the line opened on 27 July 1925, the last of Stephen's light railways to be completed. It was worked from the outset by the Southern Railway under terms agreed with the LSWR before the Grouping of 1923. However, it had managed to avoid inclusion in the Grouping and retained its identity until Nationalisation, latterly having an office at Waterloo.

South of Torrington there were stations at Hole, Hatherleigh and Petrockstow, and halts at Meeth, Dunsbear, Yarde and Watergate. Its main virtue was in providing a much shorter route between North Devon and North Cornwall than the only alternative via Okehampton. However, the train service was always very basic, timings were slow and it was one of the last outposts in the west for mixed traffic operation.

The line passed into WR control in 1963 by which time there were only two trains each way per day between Torrington and Halwill. On 1 March 1965 passenger services south of Torrington were withdrawn and Barnstaple-Torrington closed on 4 October 1966. The section between Bideford-Torrington reopened briefly between 10-22 January 1968 as an emergency measure following damage to Bideford Bridge.

In recent years the continuation of china clay traffic from Meeth has caused the northern section of the line to be retained and it has become a popular destination for enthusiasts specials. Local interests have made some progress towards reintroduction of trains between Bideford-Barnstaple with the running of a number of summer special trains. Shortage of rolling stock prevented these becoming a regular operation during the 1980 season. The ex-LSWR signalbox at Instow received attention following a campaign by local interests to prevent its demolition.

Below left: The lightweight LMS Ivatt 2-6-2Ts were popular motive power for ex-SR lines in the west of England. On 26 August 1964 No 41283 has just arrived at Torrington with the 15.15 from Barnstaple Junction, while No 41290 waits in the background with stock for the 15.55 to Halwill Junction. *P. J. Lynch*

Above: Another of the same class waits time at Yarde halt with a typical mixed train of the NDCJ line consisting of one Bulleid coach and two open wagons. *J. H. Ashton*

Below: The 16.00 Torrington-Halwill Junction pauses at Hatherleigh on 14 August 1963 with No 41283 in charge. *P. Paye*

Bude Branch

Length: 31.25 miles

The Okehampton Railway (later Devon & Cornwall) obtained powers for a line to Bude in 1865 but the powers lapsed and it was decided to build only as far as Holsworthy. The single line from a junction west of Okehampton, near Meldon, was opened on 20 January 1879. Holsworthy then became a railhead for the LSWR coach service to Bude until 10 August 1898 when the town turned out to welcome its railway. It had been built by the LSWR following the failure of a local company which obtained its powers in 1893.

There were intermediate stations at Ashbury, Halwill Junction (where the line to Padstow branched away), Dunsland Cross, Holsworthy and Whitstone & Bridgerule. The major engineering feature was Holsworhty Viaduct, of nine 50ft arches, the first of its size to be built of concrete.

Halwill Junction was an unlikely oasis of activity with little local traffic and really occurring by accident as the eventual junction of lines in four directions. It was at this remote spot that the division of the Bude and Padstow portions of the 'Atlantic Coast Express' from Waterloo took place.

The Bude branch passed into WR control in 1963 and following dieselisation and some rationalisation, it was finally closed on 3 October 1966.

Below: A classic example of the antiquated motive power with which many of the SR lines in the west of England were worked, 1897-designed 'M7' class 0-4-4T No 30320 rattles the branch train away from Bude sometime in the late 1950s. *Ian Allan Library*

Lee Moor Tramway

Length: 8.5 miles

The Lee Moor Tramway was a privately owned 'Dartmoor (4ft 6in) gauge' line built to carry china clay down to Plymouth. It was opened in 1853 and between 1899-1947 no less than three forms of traction were used to work a train over the whole length. Steam locomotives and horses were employed to haul trains, and there were two gravity-worked inclines, one of them 1.25 miles long. From 1947 until closure in 1960, during which time only the lower section was in use, horses were used.

The Lee Moor Tramway is probably best remembered for the fact that it crossed the GWR main line at Plymouth Laira on the level. Changing requirements led to closure of the northern section between Lee Moor village and Cholwich Town from 1910 and the Torycombe incline followed in 1936. The Tramway section closed during World War 2 and reopened on 8 October 1945, finally closing in 1947. From then onwards only the southern section remained in use and this lasted until 1960 when china clay production reached a level which was beyond capacity of the railway and was pumped as a slurry by pipeline to Marsh Mills.

Two 0-6-0ST steam locomotives were supplied by Peckett of Bristol in 1899. Both are still in existence, *Lee Moor No 1* being at the China Clay Industrial Museum at St Austell, and *Lee Moor No 2*, owned and restored by the Plymouth Railway Circle, is displayed at Saltram House, Plympton.

Below: The remains of the Lee Moor tramway crossing at Laira seen in the early 1960s. Part of the crossing is visible beside the signalbox.

Bottom: The Lee Moor Tramway bridge over the River Plym, with the weighhouse cottage beyond.

Plymouth-Okehampton

Length: 33.5 miles

This was the final section of the LSWR line to Plymouth, the line which put them in a position to compete for traffic against the Great Western and which led to the races of later years when the LSWR carried the passengers and the GWR the mails from the trans-Atlantic ocean liners.

The LSWR first entered Plymouth on 17 May 1876 but this was by way of the Launceston branch of the South Devon Railway (SDR) and not over their own metals. The Devon & Cornwall Railway, later part of the LSWR, reached Lydford in October 1874 and here made connection with the broad gauge SDR line through Tavistock to Plymouth. In order to run through trains it was necessary for the SDR to install mixed gauge track and they also built (at the LSWR expense) a new joint station at Plymouth North Road which was opened for traffic on 28 March 1877.

On 2 June 1890 the LSWR reached Plymouth in its own right, with completion of its independent line through Brentor, Tavistock and Bere Alston. Between Lydford and Tavistock the LSWR and SDR lines ran close together but Lydford remained the only physical connection. South of Bere Alston the LSWR acquired the metals of the Plymouth, Devonport and South Western Railway which operated the line to Callington.

On 1 July 1891 the LSWR brought into use its own station at Plymouth Friary, this having been used for freight only since 1878. For many years the layout at Plymouth was such that trains to Waterloo via the SR actually departed North Road in the opposite direction to those running to Paddignton via the GWR. Such a duplication of routes could not survive the Beeching era and it was the SR line which succumbed, largely as a result of the poor condition of the steel viaduct at Meldon, near Okehampton. The SR line to Gunnislake was retained as a branch worked from Plymouth and still has a passenger service. The line between Yeoford and Okehampton is retained for freight traffic to the granite quarry at Meldon which is still the SR source of track ballast (see Freight section). Passenger services from Exeter to Plymouth via the SR line were withdrawn in stages, Bere Alston-Okehampton on 6 May 1968 and Okehampton-Yeoford on 5 June 1972.

Above: The most imposing feature of the LSWR Exeter-Plymouth line was Meldon Viaduct, actually two single line viaducts interlaced together. In this July 1924 view, 'T9' 4-4-0 No 117, still in LSWR livery, is crossing with an up train. *H. C. Casserley*

Left: 'Black Motor' ex-LSWR '700' class 0-6-0 No 30691 in full cry passing Brentor with a Plymouth-Exeter freight. *J. C. Beckett*

Above right: SR Light Pacific No 34058 *Sir Frederick Pile* waits at the rebuilt Plymouth North Road station with an up stopping train on 5 November 1958. *B. A. Butt*

Right: Although it is hauling two autotrailers, '57xx' 0-6-0PT No 3705 is not push-pull fitted. It is here seen at the SR Plymouth Friary station on 30 August 1945, probably on the Yealmpton branch train. *H. C. Casserley*

Above: A panoramic view of the SR main line west of Bere Alston with an unidentified 'West Country' class 4-6-2 making its way towards Plymouth with a stopping train. *B. A. Butt*

Below: In a classic Devonshire scene, 'Battle of Britain' class 4-6-2 No 34070 *Manston* approaches Tavistock with the 11.50 Plymouth-Exeter on 29 April 1962. *J. C. Beckett*

Padstow Branch *Length:* 49.5 miles

The Launceston, Bodmin and Wadebridge Junction Railway was incorporated in 1864 to form a link to the Bodmin & Wadebridge line and with powers to extend to Truro. Its powers lapsed, however, and it was not until 1882 that the LSWR began to bridge the gap between its system and the little Bodmin line.

On 22 August 1882 the North Cornwall Railway, promoted by the LSWR, obtained its act for a line from Halwill Junction to Launceston and Padstow. Times were hard and construction was slow, the Halwill-Launceston section opening to traffic on 21 July 1886. It was six more years before Tresmeer was reached on 28 July 1893. Almost 13 years after the Act was passed, Wadebridge was reached on 1 June 1895 and the section from Wadebridge along the Camel estuary to Padstow opened on 27 March 1899. There were intermediate stations at Ashwater, Tower Hill, Launceston, Egloskerry, Tresmeer, Otterham, Camelford, Port Isaac Road and St Kew Highway.

At Delabole the coming of the railway brought prosperity with the development of the local slate quarry, the largest in the world. Its owners contributed 0.75 miles of the trackbed without charge and the new railway provided a fine view into the huge hole formed by the quarry workings. Launceston also provided substantial traffic and as late as 1957 the annual figures showed 750 containers of meat and 623 wagons of cattle originating there.

The Southern Railway built a new fish station at Padstow between the wars, and coal, empty boxes, ice and up to 1,000 wagon loads of fish were handled during the season. At Wadebridge, junction for the lines to Bodmin and Wenford Bridge and the connection to the GWR, up to 50 trains per day would be handled. However the decline had set in before the Beeching Report of 1963 and Padstow lost its freight service before the line closed to passengers from 30 January 1967 and the track was lifted with almost indecent haste. Wadebridge Quay continued to function until 1973 served by the line from Bodmin Road.

Below: The 01.15 from Waterloo, three through coaches plus several vans, coasts into Port Isaac Road behind 'N' class 2-6-0 No 31840 on 31 May 1960. *J. H. Aston*

Bottom: Three celebrated survivors of a much earlier motive power era were the Beattie 2-4-0 well tanks of the '0298' class, three of which were retained to work the Wenford Bridge china clay branch from Bodmin. Here, No 30586, built 1874 and subsequently rebuilt on three occasions, is working as station pilot at Wadebridge. This was the only member of the trio which was not preserved.

Above: This picture surely sums up the ex-SR lines in North Cornwall — the so-called 'withered arm'. A vintage 4-4-0, 'T9' No 30711, crosses Little Petherick Creek on the Camel estuary with the two-coach 14.28 Wadebridge-Padstow on 26 April 1954.

Below: The station at Padstow occupied a picturesque setting beside the Camel estuary. In early BR days, with much of the stock in carmine and cream livery, 'T9' 4-4-0 No 30712, still in SR colours, hurries away from the terminus with a stopping train to Launceston. *B. A. Butt*

Helston Branch

Length: 8.75 miles

The branch to Helston was the last section of line to complete the railway map in western Cornwall, but it was not for want of effort, proposals having been made in 1845, 1864 and 1872. A further scheme, put forward in 1879 met with more success and the Helston Railway Act received Royal Assent on 9 July 1880. The line was to be standard (4ft 8.5in) gauge and the first sod was cut on 22 March 1882. On 9 May 1887 the first train ran into Helston carrying some 50 passengers.

The branch joined the GWR main line at Gwinear Road and intermediate stations were provided at Praze and Nancegollan. The latter possessed the only passing loop on the single track branch, and was rebuilt in 1937 with two platform roads and a passing loop. Truthall halt was opened on 3 July 1905, changing its name to Truthall platform a year later. Helston station, the most southerly station in Britain, is perhaps best remembered as the focus of the first motor bus service to operate in connection with the trains. The service between Helston and The Lizard commenced on 17 August 1903 using a 22-seater vehicle acquired from the Lynton & Barnstaple Railway. The L&BR had attempted to start a similar service in North Devon but disposed of the vehicle following a prosecution for 'speeding' at 8mph.

The Royal Cornwall Show was sometimes held at Helston and this brought a considerable influx of traffic. In addition, just after World War 2 special trains were operated for service personnel. Otherwise, the line suffered from the usual fluctuations of seasonal traffic experienced by West Country lines and generated little traffic of its own. It closed to passengers on 3 November 1962, the last train being drawn by NBL Class 22 diesel No D6312, one of a class which had taken over workings on the line. Freight traffic survived until October 1964 and the track was lifted during the following year.

Below: '45xx' 2-6-2T No 4564 gets away from Helston with the 16.15 train to Gwinear Road conveying a fish van and a container ahead of the passenger coaches. *C. S. Heaps*

Portreath and Tresavean Goods Branches

These two freight lines diverged from the GWR main line between Carn Brea and Redruth. The Portreath line was opened in December 1837 to serve the busy harbour at Portreath. Its main traffic was in coal and ore and by 1846 it had become necessary to add an inner basin to the harbour, because it was not uncommon to find as many as 20 vessels in harbour at any one time. By 1930 all such activity had ceased and the branch was closed on 1 April 1938. The Tresavean branch, built to serve the mining industry, was closed in 1932. Several other Cornish branches which have never supported a public passenger service continue to thrive. They include those from St Dennis to Meledor Mill and Burngullow to Drinnick Mill.

Main Lines

Western Region Main Line

The first GWR plan for a line into Devon and Cornwall entailed a junction with the London-Bristol line at Bath, giving access to Plymouth via Wells, Glastonbury, Taunton and Exeter. However, the plan was pre-empted by the Bristol & Exeter Railway's proposal for a line linking the cities named in its title. The first section of the B&ER, to Bridgwater, was opened on 14 June 1841 together with the branch to Weston-super-Mare. There was no public ceremony to mark the event, and indeed the B&ER was so short of money that the new section was leased immediately to the Great Western so that precious capital could be saved for further construction work.

Under the terms of the lease the B&ER had to complete construction of the line to Exeter, and it did so in stages, opening to Taunton on 1 July 1842 and finally reaching Exeter on 1 May 1844.

In October 1843 a prospectus for the Plymouth, Devonport and Exeter Railway was issued but by the time its Bill had been deposited before Parliament in 1844 the title had been changed to the South Devon Railway. The Bill had an easy passage through both Houses, receiving the Royal Assent on 4 July 1844. The SDR route involved a number of long climbs and descents and it was felt that the locomotives available at the time would be incapable of handling the traffic without resort to expensive double-heading. On the advice of its engineer, I. K. Brunel, the SDR Board decided to adopt the novel atmospheric system of traction.

The atmospheric system had been in use on the Kingstown and Dalkey Railway in Ireland, but the SDR route was by far the most ambitious application of the system then contemplated. The system employed a 15in diameter pipe laid between the rails, the pipe having a continuous slit along the top. A piston inside the pipe was connected, through the slot, to the underside of a special vehicle attached to the front of the train. A leather flap laid in a trough of tallow sealed the slit in front of and behind the piston. At intervals along the line stationary pump engines were provided and these exhausted the air from the pipe ahead of the piston. Atmospheric pressure behind the piston and the vacuum ahead of it, forced the piston to move along the pipe, drawing the train with it.

The first section, from Exeter to Teignmouth, opened to passengers on 30 May 1846, and stationary engine houses were provided at three-mile intervals. The section onward to Newton (known as Newton Abbot from 1877) opened on 1 May 1847 and to Totnes on 20 July. Locomotives were used initially as there had been difficulties in completing the atmospheric engine houses in time, but the first atmospheric passenger train operated on 13 September 1847. Almost immediately the system experienced problems, but in spite of these a maximum speed of 68mph was attained with a 28ton train. The first winter of operation showed up some insurmountable problems — rats were found to eat the tallow-soaked leather, water froze in the pipes, and repeated freezing of the leather made it brittle and prevented effective sealing of the pipe. After eight months of operation, virtually all the leather required replacement, and Brunel was obliged to abandon the system in the face of mounting repair costs. Steam locomotives took over all train workings from September 1848. The system has been called 'Brunel's Folly', but in fairness to the engineer it must have seemed to offer great advantages over the feeble and temperamental steam locomotives of the time, while its protection of the environment is something which would surely have found favour today. Even the pump engine houses were carefully designed, looking for all the world like Italian chapels, each of their chimneys disguised as a tower and topped with a mock campanile (bell tower).

By 5 May 1848 the line had been completed through to Plymouth and on 18 December the same year the branch from Newton to Torquay was opened. The Plymouth terminus, between Union Street and Millbay Road, was brought into use on 2 April 1849.

In 1835 the Cornwall Railway placed before Parliament a bill for a line following an inland route between Exeter and Falmouth, but it was not approved. A later bill of 1846 sought for a line engineered by Brunel, crossing the River Tamar at Plymouth and proceeding via St Germans to join the course of its ill-fated predecessor. It received the Royal Assent on 3 August 1846 and work commenced on the Truro-St Austell section. Progress was hampered by a shortage of funds and the CR was eventually leased jointly to the GWR, SDR and B&ER. By February 1859 the Truro-St Germans section was virtually complete, and the bridge over the Tamar was nearing completion. It was designed by Brunel, but he was closely involved in his work on the PS *Great Eastern* and most of the bridge construction was left to R. P. Brereton. Brunel personally supervised the final positioning of the first main span, watched by a huge audience which maintained a perfect silence while the final instructions were given. The job was completed with absolute precision and the engineer was hailed as a hero, finally redeeming himself for the 'atmospheric disaster' in the eyes of the people of the west. The bridge cost £225,000, and the first major repairs were carried out in 1960 when strengthened bracing was installed.

The section of line from St Germans to Saltash was the

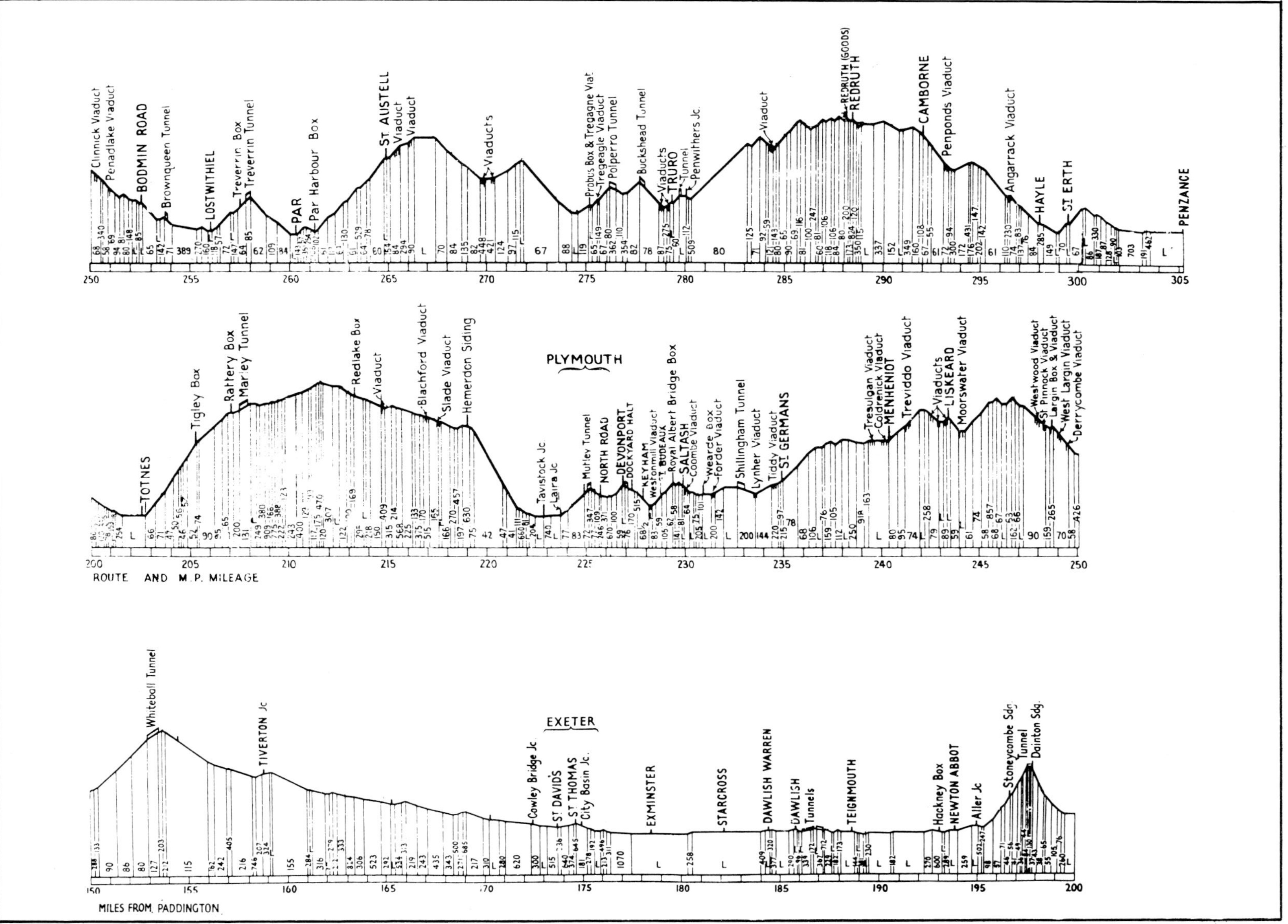

Clinnick Viaduct
Penadlake Viaduct
BODMIN ROAD
Brownqueen Tunnel
LOSTWITHIEL
Treverrin Box
Treverrin Tunnel
PAR
Par Harbour Box
ST AUSTELL
Viaduct
Viaduct
Viaducts
Probus Box & Tregagne Viat.
Tregeagle Viaduct
Polperro Tunnel
Buckshead Tunnel
Viaducts
TRURO
Tunnel
Penwithers Jc.
Viaduct
REDRUTH (GOODS)
REDRUTH
CAMBORNE
Penponds Viaduct
Angarrack Viaduct
HAYLE
ST ERTH
PENZANCE
250   255   260   265   270   275   280   285   290   295   300   305
TOTNES
Tigley Box
Rattery Box
Marley Tunnel
Redlake Box
Viaduct
Blachford Viaduct
Slade Viaduct
Hemerdon Siding
PLYMOUTH
Tavistock Jc.
Laira Jc.
Mutley Tunnel
NORTH ROAD
DEVONPORT
DOCKYARD HALT
KEYHAM
Westonmill Viaduct
ST BUDEAUX
Royal Albert Bridge Box
SALTASH
Coombe Viaduct
Wearde Box
Forder Viaduct
Shillingham Tunnel
Lynher Viaduct
Tiddy Viaduct
ST GERMANS
Tresulgan Viaduct
Coldrenick Viaduct
MENHENIOT
Treviddo Viaduct
Viaducts
LISKEARD
Moorswater Viaduct
Westwood Viaduct
St Pinnock Viaduct
Largin Box & Viaduct
West Largin Viaduct
Derrycombe Viaduct
200   205   210   215   220   225   230   235   240   245   250
ROUTE   AND   M.P. MILEAGE
Whiteball Tunnel
Tiverton Jc.
EXETER
Cowley Bridge Jc.
ST DAVID'S
ST THOMAS
City Basin Jc.
EXMINSTER
STARCROSS
DAWLISH WARREN
DAWLISH
Tunnels
TEIGNMOUTH
Hackney Box
NEWTON ABBOT
Aller Jc.
Stoneycombe Sdg.
Tunnel
Dainton Sdg.
150   155   160   165   170   175   180   185   190   195   200
MILES FROM PADDINGTON.

last to be completed, on 11 April 1859, and on 2 May HRH The Prince Consort opened the bridge to which his name had been given. the line opened to passenger traffic two days later. In addition to the Royal Albert Bridge, there were 34 timber viaducts on the Cornwall Railway, built to a standard Brunel design. They had masonry piers built to a point 35ft below track level, the spans being formed on a fan of standard timber frames. These made use of the abundant Cornish carpentry skills and had the advantage that any frame section could be easily replaced when repairs were needed. The last of the main line viaducts, at Stomehouse Pool, was replaced with an orthodox viaduct in 1908.

In 1834 the Hayle Railway had obtained an Act to construct a line from Hayle Foundry to Tresavean Mire with branches to Porteath and Redruth. The 17 miles of line opened in 1837/8, mainly for freight traffic, with passengers being conveyed in open mineral wagons. The West Cornwall Railway Bill of 1844 proposed to extend the Hayle Railway to connect with Truro and Penzance, but Parliament refused to sanction it, feeling that a better route could be found. A suitable alternative route was found and the Hayle Railway was subsequently purchased by the WCR. Powers granted in 1850 enabled the line to be built to standard gauge, but completion was further delayed when a ship carrying the rails from South Wales sank in a storm. The line was opened from Penzance to Redruth on 11 March 1852 and through to Truro on 25 August

The break of gauge at Truro caused difficulties and on 1 July 1866 the WCR was leased to the big three broad gauge companies, who set about installing mixed gauge track, the first broad gauge train working through to Penzance on 1 March 1867. From November 1871 until the abolition of the broad gauge it was possible to find the novelty of mixed gauge goods trains conveying wagons of both gauges in the same train.

By the 1870s the speed and comfort advantages of the broad gauge were being equalled by the standard gauge companies, while difficulties at break of gauge points had reached crisis level. Mixed gauge had gradually spread through the system and in 1891 the GWR Board decided to abolish the broad gauge. The final sections of broad gauge in the West Country were converted in a meticulously timed operation on the weekend on 20-23 May. Some 213 miles of track were dealt with and 3,700 men were brought in to assist the regular gangs. The last down broad gauge train on 20 May 1892 was the 10.15 Paddington-Penzance 'Cornishman', and the last up train the 21.45 from Penzance. The latter carried an inspector whose duty it was to ensure that all broad gauge stock had been moved east to Exeter. The night mail train on the Sunday was booked to Plymouth via the LSWR route and reached Penzance on schedule at 04.40, over the re-gauged track.

West of Exeter most of the main line was single track, and as traffic increased it became necessary to widen earthworks and install double track. The section between Bodmin Road and Lostwithiel was the first to be so treated, in July 1893 and the last between St Erth and Marazion in June 1929.

The Great Western Railway's route to Devon and Cornwall via Bristol earned it the uncomplimentary title of the 'Great Way Round' and in due course the completion of the route via Westbury to Cogload Junction near Taunton provided a more direct line. From the early years of the present century much of the Paddington-West of England traffic was routed via the Westbury line and the 10.30 departure from Paddington was destined to become the west's most famous train. Skilful marketing and publicity created a legend around the 'Cornish Riviera Express', known often as the '10.30 Limited', due to its all-reserved seat accommodation. It was always provided with top-ranking motive power, at first with 'Castle' and then 'King' class 4-6-0s and in BR days with the latest 'Warship' class diesel-hydraulics and latterly with Class 50s and the latest high speed trains.

During the 1950s the revival of GWR traditions, including the painting of some coaches in chocolate and cream, saw the re-introduction of named express trains and some of the best-known examples worked into the West of England — the 'Torbay Express' from Paddington to Kingswear, the 'Royal Duchy' from Paddington to Penzance calling at all the major Cornish stations, the 'Mayflower' from Paddington to Plymouth, the 'Cornishman' from Wolverhampton to Kingswear/Penzance, and the 'Devonian' from Bradford to Paignton. All these have since ceased to carry their names, although for a while there was a concerted effort to promote the 'Mayflower' as a high-speed, executive service.

High speed trains were introduced on the West of England line in 1979 following their considerable success in boosting traffic on the South Wales and Bristol routes. Additional Class 253 units were ordered but the change from Brush electrical equipment to GEC proved problematic and delayed their entry into service. Some Paddington-Bristol services reverted to locomotive haulage to release IC125 units to cover West of England diagrams.

From time to time there have been fears for the future of rail services west of Plymouth and indeed all of the remaining branch lines have been threatened with closure at some time. However, the heavy repairs to the Royal Albert Bridge carried out in 1960 and the introduction of high speed trains are a positive commitment to continued rail service in the west, and coupled perhaps with extension of the 'park and ride' system, they suggest a brighter future for the rail routes in Devon and Cornwall.

Top right: Starting out on the steep climb from Exeter St Davids to Central, 'Z' class 0-8-0T No 30955 assists '700' 0-6-0 No 30327 with the 11.35 Meldon-Exmouth Junction goods on 15 August 1960. The train was banked in the rear by 'Z' No 30956. *M. J. Fox*

Bottom right: This view of No 25.223 heading a trip working to Exmouth out of Exeter St Davids clearly shows the steepness of the climb towards Central station. *Brian Morrison*

Top right: During the mid-1980s the establishment of new power signalboxes at Exeter and Westbury will bring virtually all the WR lines east of Plymouth under multiple aspect colour light signalling. The manual signalbox at Exeter St Davids, seen here in July 1976, will be among those closed. *Brian Morrison*

Centre right: A panoramic view of Exeter St Davids with a down freight consisting mainly of empty china clay wagons, making its way round the avoiding line. The main platforms are on the right, and the remains of the locomotive shed (code 83C) are on the extreme left. *Brian Morrison*

Below: A flashback to steam days with a typical SR local train arriving behind 'N' 2-6-0 No 31846. This train is bound for Exeter Central, and the date is 10 August 1953. One of the delights of train-spotting at St Davids was that the station announcer would often describe arriving motive power in some detail as the train approached. *A. Mayor*

Above: Summer Saturday trains from Brighton to Exeter are often worked by pairs of Class 33 locomotives. On 26 July 1980 Nos 33.051/8 head the train from Brighton into Exeter St Davids off the incline from Central. *Les Bertram*

Below: Relaxing momentarily after its exertions over the steep banks of South Devon, No 50.044 (since named *Exeter*) rumbles over the River Exe with the 09.35 Paignton–Paddington. *Brian Morrison*

Above: The introduction of IC125 services between Paddington-Penzance in the autumn of 1979 changed the visual image of railways in the west. Here, unit No 253.030 leaves Exeter St Davids with the 11.08 Penzance-Paddington on 26 July 1980. *Les Bertram*

Left: Beyond Exeter, the former South Devon Railway main line follows the Exe valley to the coast, which it reaches at Starcross. In this 1979 view of a Plymouth-Cardiff dmu passing Starcross the roof and tower of the former atmospheric railway pump house can be seen. This is the largest surviving relic of Brunel's disastrous scheme, and the fine Italianate building is now in a state of disrepair. The truncated tower in fact disguised a chimney and was originally topped by a mock campanile. *Les Bertram*

Below left: From Dawlish Warren to Teignmouth the line follows the coast closely, frequently occupying a narrow ledge between the red cliffs and the shore. Much of this seawall provides a promenade with a superb view of the trains and in this view Collett '2251' class 0-6-0 No 2208 rattles a short van train along near Dawlish, bound for Newton Abbot. *E. D. Bruton*

Top: Dawlish is a popular resort and its station is right on the seafront. The screaming Valentas of an IC125 unit accelerating the 11.20 Paddington-Paignton away from Dawlish attract scarcely a glance from holidaymakers in this 4 June 1980 view. *G. A. Watt*

Above: This stretch of line is periodically subjected to damage by pounding seas and it is a creditable performance that delays of only a few minutes were caused by these conditions on 27 December 1979 as No 45.023 *The Royal Pioneer Corps* gets a dousing with the 07.23 Cardiff-Plymouth. *M. J. Collins*

Left: The same location seen a few months earlier in August 1979 with a fully-fitted freight train rattling along the seawall behind No 31.118/24. *A. O. Wynn*

Top right: At each headland the railway cuts through tunnels, as here at Horse Cove, just west of Dawlish. Class 46 No 46.056 heads the 07.47 Penzance-Liverpool into the tunnels on 6 July 1979. *Brian Morrison*

Centre right: As the railway turns inland through Teignmouth station it is crossed by a steeply inclined lattice-girder bridge which has been a popular location for railway photographers since the days of the broad gauge. In this 1959 view LMS '8F' 2-8-0 No 48424 provides unusual motive power for a Tavistock-Rogerstone freight. *S. Creer*

Below: The 08.57 Paddington-Paignton approaches Newton Abbot behind No 47.111 on 2 July 1979. Newton Abbot race course is visible on the left. *Brian Morrison*

Above: A flashback to steam days with 'Hall' 4–6–0 No 5967 *Bickmarsh Hall* piloting 'Castle' 4–6–0 No 5058 *Earl of Clancarty* on the 11.30 Paddington-Plymouth. *J. F. Loader*

Below: There are fewer locomotives and signals, and the power station chimneys have gone, but otherwise this 1980 view of the same location shows remarkably little change. No 47.479 is departing with the 08.40 Liverpool-Penzance and on the right yellow-painted railway carriages belonging to fellow railway publishers David & Charles Ltd are visible. *G. A. Watt*

Top: The new-look up 'Cornish Riviera Express' formed by IC125 unit No 253.008 passes Aller Junction, south of Newton Abbot. The diverging line to Torquay and Paignton is visible behind the rear power car.   *M. S. Wilkins*

Above: IC125 units are now a familiar sight on Paignton services. On 9 June 1980 No 253.025 is seen passing Holliecombe Bay near Torquay with the 11.20 Paddington-Paignton.   *G. A. Watt*

Right: Four years earlier, on 21 August 1976, the photographer captured No 47.112 getting away from sunny Torquay with the 10.30. Paddington-Paignton.   *Les Bertram*

Left: Torquay has a fine station built of local stone and the mild climate has enabled exotic shrubs to grow on the platform. *G. A. Watt*

Below: A sunny 5 August 1961 sees NBL Type 2 Diesel No D6332 resting between station pilot duties as 'Warship' No D838 *Rapid* arrives with a down train. *I. G. Holt*

Bottom: One of the first West of England trains to receive Mk 2 air conditioned coaching stock was the 07.22 (SO) Paddington-Paignton, here seen between Torquay and Paignton on 28 August 1976. *Les Bertram*

TORBAY STEAM RAILWAY
PAIGNTON
0V42
MODEL RAILWAY
EXHIBITION
TORBAY STEAM RAILWAY

REGENT
British Rail Paignton
Members of the
public must not
enter the station
by this route
Failure to comply
with the ruling
can result in
prosecution and
a fine of £200

Above left: BR services on the former Kingswear line now operate only to and from Paignton, the section onwards to Kingswear having been taken over by the Dart Valley Railway and operated as the Torbay Steam Railway. In this 1975 view No 47.129 is waiting to leave with the 16.38 service to Newton Abbot. *P. D. Hawkins*

Left: Five years later, and the changes are obvious. The platform ramps have been altered to accommodate lifting barriers protecting the adjacent level crossing. No 45.058 is starting the 16.40 to Exeter on 6 June 1980. *G. A. Watt*

Above: Returning to the main line, beyond Aller Junction the line climbs to Dainton Tunnel, the summit being reached just outside the western portal. The South Devon banks have always presented a formidable obstacle to trains, and 'County' class 4-6-0 No 1010 *County of Caernarvon* makes a fine sight at the head of a Goodrington Sands-Plymouth train on 7 August 1956. *T. E. Williams*

Centre right: Modern motive power is less daunted by the gradients and IC125 unit No 253.007 snakes through the curves at the approach to Dainton tunnel with the up 'Cornish Riviera' on 26 May 1981. The sign board warns down freight trains conveying more than 35 wagons to stop dead before commencing the descent. *M. S. Wilkins*

Bottom right: An unusual view of Dainton summit. No 46.039 goes over the top with the 15.00 Truro-Ince & Elton UKF fertiliser empties formed of modern special purpose vans on 27 April 1981. *C. F. Beatson*

Right: Totnes station was the last main line station to retain a Brunel-pattern overall roof, and this was removed during the 1930s. More recently the station was damaged by fire and the remaining structures are an unattractive clutter. On 7 March 1978, No 50.005 (since named *Collingwood*) on the 08.05 Bristol-Penzance overtakes a trio of light engines returning to Plymouth Laira depot. *M. S. Wilkins*

Below: The intermediate stations between Totnes and Plymouth have been closed and little now remains at most of the sites. One of the landmarks on this section is the viaduct at Ivybridge, but the Brunel 'chalet' station building visible on the left in this 1929 view has now gone.

Bottom: A scene from the Western Region's golden age of diesel-hydraulics and brown and cream coaches. Nos D6314 and D801 *Vanguard* descend Rattery bank with the up 'Cornish Riviera' and pass No D829 *Magpie* with a down van train. *R. E. Toop*

Top: The reconstruction of Plymouth North Road station during the late 1950s was a much publicised event accompanied by the re-issue of some early photographs of the station, such as this view taken on 27 February 1928. *BR*

Above: Plymouth area local services were for many years worked by 0-6-0PTs and autocoaches. This splendidly atmospheric shot taken at midnight on a December night in 1959 shows a typical train worked by '64xx' 0-6-0PT No 6400 in the final months before diesel units took over. *J. R. Smith*

Left: A quiet moment on 23 August 1977 as a Class 08 shunter trundles a local trip working through North Road station. *D. Kimber*

Top: The band played 'See the conquering hero comes' as Brunel supervised the positioning of the first span of his magnificent Royal Albert Bridge across the Tamar at Saltash. When the bridge was completed in 1859 the dying engineer was wheeled across his masterpiece in an open wagon and for 100 years it formed the major physical link between Devon and Cornwall at this point. Road traffic was faced with a journey many miles inland to avoid long summer queues for the Saltash Corporation Ferry which is seen in this view waiting to leave the Devon shore. The warships visible in the background were a familiar part of the scene until the relentless reductions of the British fleet in recent years. Even so, Plymouth is still home base for many famous warships whose names are now reflected on the diesel locomotives which ply their trade across Brunel's bridge. Many ships are laid up in the backwaters of the Tamar, and quite recently the aircraft carrier *Ark Royal* was decommissioned and stripped of useful materials at Plymouth before breaking up. *Studio St Ives*

Above and right: Each span of the Royal Albert Bridge obtains its strength from the oval wrought iron tube (visible at top of illustration) together with the suspension chains formed of flat wrought iron links. The deck is suspended from the chains and braced to the tube with vertical supports which were strengthened in the 1960s to accommodate heavier trains. This is the only major modification carried out since the bridge was built. It carries only a single track, which was originally broad gauge. *Ian Allan Library; R. T. Coxon*

Top left: The Tamar road bridge, opened in 1960 overshadows the Royal Albert Bridge and it has replaced the ferry, although a toll is still charged for crossing it. Some motorists still prefer to travel by rail, and Motorail services from Kensington Olympia to St Austell convey holidaymakers and their cars to Cornwall avoiding the traffic jams. No 47.074 heads a Motorail train from St Austell over the Royal Albert Bridge, approaching the signalbox at the end of the single track section on 14 July 1979. *A. J. Whitehouse*

Centre left: The telephoto lens takes us close to the western portal of the bridge and the ladders and inspection walkway over the top of the tube are clearly visible. *Brian Morrison*

Below: A Tamar panorama of steam days with a Penzance-Newton Abbot stopping train crossing Combe Viaduct on the approach to Saltash station. Below the spans of the Brunel bridge, the route of the SR main line to Okehampton and Exeter is clearly visible. *R. E. Vincent*

Above: Further down the cost No D829 *Magpie* heads the down 'Royal Duchy', one of several named trains introduced during the 1950s. In the background warship spotters will recognise two carriers of the 'Hermes' class. *J. C. Beckett*

Below: Forder viaduct near Saltash, seen from an unusual viewpoint. *Les Bertram*

Above: Liskeard station is situated on a hillside and is reached by crossing deep valleys on either side. No 50.030 *Repulse*, one of the Class 50s which adopted the tradition of 'warship' names begun by previous WR classes, heads the 13.59 Penzance-Bristol into Liskeard on 18 July 1978. *Brian Morrison*

Centre left: Moorswater viaduct, just west of Liskeard is probably the most well known of the West Country viaducts. The pillars of the original Brunel timber structure are visible in this view of '45xx' 2-6-2T No 4505 running back from Moorswater china clay sidings with a brake van on 31 August 1954. *R. C. Riley*

Bottom left: The sidings and locomotive shed at Moorswater seen from the viaduct in 1958. The old line to Caradon ran to the right of the shed. *R. Steiber*

Above: Since this photograph of 'Hall' 4-6-0 No 4908 *Broome Hall* starting the down 'Cornishman' from Bodmin Road was taken on 11 June 1956 almost everything has changed. There is no more steam in Cornwall, red and cream coaches have gone although plenty of Mk 1 vehicles survive at present, and the Cornwall Railway timber buildings have been replaced with noteless modern structures. *M. Mensing*

Centre right: Locomotive withdrawals during 1981 made heavy inroads into the ranks of Class 46s which had for a few years reigned supreme in the far west. On 8 May 1976 No 46.007 blasts out of Brown Queen tunnel an up train. *H. T. Heyl*

Bottom right: High speed trains have quickly become accepted as part of the scene in the West Country where their rapid acceleration rather than high maximum speed has proved valuable in reducing journey times. The up 'Cornish Riviera' formed by No 253.019 passes picturesque countryside near Bodmin Road on 1 October 1979. *Les Bertram*

Above: Lostwithiel station's original Cornwall Railway buildings are the last of their kind of the main line and their recent history is a sad story. After the structures on one platform were demolished, the remaining buildings and goods shed were 'listed' by the Department of Environment to prevent further destruction. Arrears of maintenance since the structures were last painted in 1956 allowed them to fall into disrepair and in **1981 Restormel Council gave its consent to their demolition.** *Brian Morrison*

Bottom : A flashback to steam days with '14xx' 0-4-2T No 1419 waiting to leave Lostwithiel with the 18.10 train to Fowey. *P. Q. Treloar*

Above: Par station is now the only junction for passenger services to Newquay and on 2 September 1978 No 50.035 *Ark Royal* was seen coming off the branch with the 10.00 (SO) Newquay-Newcastle through train. *Les Bertram*

Below: The 07.30 Paddington-Penzance, formed of air conditioned Mk 2 stock and headed by a Class 47 locomotive, is about to plunge into Treverrin tunnel on 7 April 1977. *Les Bertram*

Top: The busy little station at St Austell still retained some of its Great Western atmosphere in this 1978 view as No 50.020 *Revenge* brings the 12.24 Penzance-Paddington to a halt. *Les Bertram*

Above: The ivy-covered piers of the original Brunel timber viaduct are visible in this view of Gover viaduct near St Austell. *Les Bertram*

Left: The area around St Austell is the centre of the Cornish china clay industry, and although the station at Burngullow has all but disappeared, the point remains a junction for the branch to china clay works sidings at Drinnick Mill. A typical china clay factory (known as dries), with sheeted wagons in the adjacent siding is seen in this view of No 47.496 passing Burngullow with the 09.35 Paddington-Penzance on 30 August 1978. *Les Bertram*

Right: There was plenty of activity at Truro on 19 May 1959, with no less than 10 locomotives present as '4575' 2-6-2T No 5500 approaches on the up line with a typical freight working. *M. Mensing*

Below: The splendid stone viaduct at Chacewater is crossed by No 50.038 at the head of the 12.20 Penzance-Paddington on 16 July 1977. *P. D. Hawkins*

Top right: Tin mining was once a major industry in Cornwall, but the ore was difficult to extract and therefore expensive so its fortunes fluctuated with world demand. Flooding of the shafts was always a problem and the Cornish mine engineers were among the first to make widespread use of steam pumping engines. Today the derelict engine houses provide a gaunt monument to 18th century ingenuity. No 45.006 heads a short train of cement hopper wagons past the remains of an engine house between Redruth and Truro. *G. W. Morrison*

Bottom right: The fireman leans from the cab of '4575' 2-6-2T No 4588 with the Helston branch single line staff ready to deliver it to the signalman at Gwinear Road as the 16.10 branch train arrives. *M. Mensing*

Top: The BR Standard 'Britannia' class 4–6–2s were the only Pacifics to work regularly into Cornwall and on 10 April 1952 No 70024 *Vulcan* had charge of the down 'Cornish Riviera'. It is entering Gwinear Road station over the wide level crossing, and in the background a freight train is waiting in the yard and a Helston branch train is approaching, yet this once busy junction has now disappeared. *B. A. Butt*

Above: On a stormy 9 April 1960 'County' 4–6–0 No 1018 *County of Leicester* pounds over Angarrack Viaduct between Hayle and Gwinear Road with the 13.55 Penzance-Truro. *P. Q. Treloar*

Right: Hayle station has been much modernised but at the time of this photograph on 10 July 1976 it still retained a fine signalbox. No 47.063 is arriving with the 08.40 Plymouth-Penzance. *P. D. Hawkins*

Above: In the last months of the Great Western Railway, recently built 'County' 4-6-0 No 1023 *County of Oxford* heads the 17.00 stopping train to Penzance over Hayle viaduct on 20 May 1947. *B. A. Butt*

Right: St Erth is the junction for the branch to St Ives which is the second track to the right of the locomotive in this 1975 view of No 50.013 departing with the 14.10 Penzance-Paddington. *Brian Morrison*

Top right: Although the village it serves is quite small, St Erth is an important railhead for the surrounding area and it was a busy centre for milk traffic until West Country milk trains ceased operating in 1980. A milk train for Acton was being marshalled by Class 52 No D1013 *Western Ranger* in St Erth sidings on 30 July 1975. *Brian Morrison*

Centre right: Camping coaches available for rent from BR were once a popular way of having an off-beat self-catering holiday in many of the rail-served resorts. Few camping coaches now survive and they are retained for use by rail staff. The six former Pullman cars sited at the remains of Marazion station are now the largest collection of their type, and were built in the 1920s. It was once a condition of hire, that holidaymakers had to reach their camping coach by rail, clearly at Marazion this is no longer possible. *Les Bertram*

Below: From Marazion the line skirts the shore of Mounts Bay for the last miles into the terminus at Penzance. A quiet moment between trains in the late afternoon of 9 July 1953 finds 'Castle' No 5023 *Brecon Castle* at the head of a short milk train. Behind it can be seen the vans of the immortal overnight Travelling Post Office train which even in the 1980s retains its old name the 'Great Western TPO'. *C. R. L. Coles*

Top: Three years later and '43xx' 2-6-0 No 6397 stands at the head of a stopping train to Truro while '94xx' 0-6-0PT No 8492 departs with a through train to Falmouth.   *B. A. Butt*

Above: A modern scene at Long Rock, the former Penzance carriage sidings, where a new maintenance shed has been constructed to service high speed trains. On 23 July 1978 No 50.009 *Conqueror* was passing with the 10.15 to Paddington.   *Les Bertram*

Right: Looking down from the concourse at Penzance in 1966. 'Warship' No D828 *Magnificent* has just arrived with a stopping train from Plymouth.   *Chris Leigh*

Secondary Lines

Southern Region Main Line

The former Southern Railway route from Waterloo to the West of England is now sadly reduced to the role of a secondary main line. Set against the picture of IC125s on the busy WR main line, the SR route supports just seven trains each way per day between Waterloo and Exeter. Long stretches of the line have been reduced to single track, and beyond Sherborne it is now under the control of the Western Region. Indeed, it is the WR which supplies the rolling stock and Class 50 locomotives with which the service is operated.

Between the former Chard Junction station and Axminster, the line passed from Somerset into Devon before crossing the River Axe into Dorset and then re-crossing it back into Devon again. The first train had worked through from Salisbury to Exeter on 18 July 1860 following some five years of construction work. The London & South Western Railway had eventually settled upon this route rather than the more circuitous proposed route via Dorchester, probably due largely to the efforts of the engineer Joseph Locke who was also Member of Parliament for Honiton.

Despite the need for some long ascents and a good deal of climbing around the hills, the route was well engineered. Just after Axminster, at the $146\frac{1}{4}$ milepost, down trains face the start of the eight mile long Honiton bank. Its last 4.5miles are continuously at 1 in 80 and after the site of Seaton Junction station, the summit is reached inside the 1,353yd Honiton Tunnel. The line then descends for nearly five miles, through Honiton at 1 in 80-100 to the site of Sidmouth Junction station. The descent continues more gently through Whimple and Broad Clyst until climbing commences again at 1 in 100 through Pinhoe on the outskirts of Exeter.

With the site of Exmouth Junction motive power depot on the right, a 263yd tunnel is entered before arrival at Exeter Central, the former LSWR station. From here, trains continuing to Plymouth were obliged to run via the GWR Exeter St Davids station and to reach this there is a sharply curved descent at 1 in 37. Most up trains required assistance from St Davids to Central and for many years the curious 'Z' class 0-8-0s were stationed here for this job. Today trains from Waterloo terminate at St Davids, but in the days of through SR trains to Plymouth one would find trains via the two different routes facing in opposite directions. A glance at the map reveals that SR trains departed northwards to Plymouth via Crediton and Okehampton, while WR services to Plymouth via Newton Abbot departed southwards.

North of St Davids the former SR route diverges at Cowley Bridge Junction through Newton St Cyres and Crediton, to Yeoford Junction. Here, the branch to Barnstaple diverged northwards and the Plymouth line headed west to face an almost unbroken climb from near sea level on the banks of the Exe to 950ft at Meldon. Now, however, the Barnstaple route is the major one, with the Plymouth line remaining only as a single track freight line to the ballast quarry at Meldon.

Before leaving the SR route, mention must be made of its most famous train, the 'Atlantic Coast Express' latterly nicknamed the 'ACE'. This remarkable train included through coaches for more destinations than any other British express. Its 13 coaches comprised three for Ilfracombe, one each for Torrington, Padstow, Bude and Plymouth, two restaurant cars detached at Exeter, one coach each for Sidmouth and Exmouth, and one for stations between Salisbury and Seaton. It was a victim of the change in regional boundaries in 1963 when the WR eliminated locomotive working from most of the branches which it served and substituted diesel multiple units. The 'ACE' finished at the end of the 1964 summer timetable.

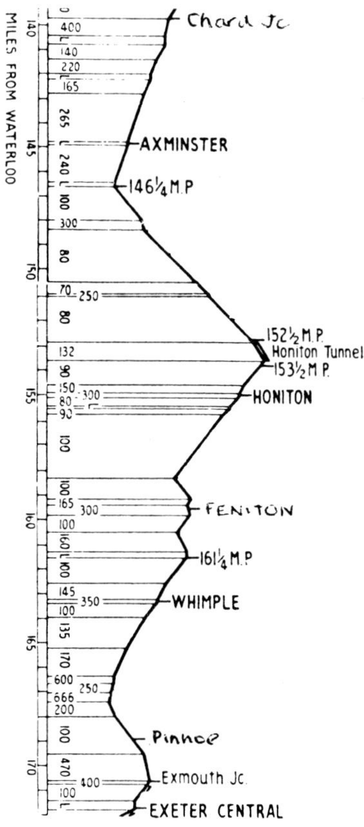

Above: Exmouth Junction-based 'S15' class 4-6-0 No 30845 ambles into Axminster trailing a long mixed freight. *J. Davenport*

Left: The much rebuilt and rationalised Honiton station seen on 26 July 1980. The 06.50 Waterloo-Exeter is passed by No 50.010 *Monarch* on the 08.23 through train from Barnstaple-Waterloo. *Les Bertram*

Below: Rebuilt 'West Country' class 4-6-2 No 34093 *Saunton* rolls down from Honiton Tunnel with an up express from the West of England on 5 September 1964. *P. Riley*

Right: Making a fine display, SR Light Pacific No 34006 *Bude* pounds up the bank from Seaton Junction towards Honiton Tunnel with a special working from Waterloo to Budleigh Salterton on 2 April 1966. *C. E. Weston*

Below: Another Light Pacific, 'West Country' class 4-6-2 No 34038 *Lynton* gets away from Exeter Central with an up train from Plymouth. The banker from St Davids is visible just to the left of the signal post. *J. Robertson*

Bottom: When the SR lines west of Wilton passed into WR control in 1963, the services to and from Waterloo were quickly dieselised with WR 'Warship' class diesel-hydraulics. On 4 September 1964 No D825 *Intrepid* restarts the last weekday 'Atlantic Coast Express' from Exeter Central en route to Waterloo. *R. W. Hawkins*

Left: Following the demise of the WR diesel-hydraulics, SR motive power returned to the Waterloo-Exeter services during the 1970s with the use of Class 33s on most trains marking the ever-declining status of the route. In this view, No 33.112 is straining all its 1,550 'horses' to drag the 14.28 Exeter St Davids-Waterloo up the 1 in 37 into Exeter Central. *Brian Morrison*

Above: The new order on the Exeter-Waterloo services is represented by this view of Class 50 Co-Co No 50.016 *Barham* arriving at Exeter Central with the 11.43 Exeter St Davids-Waterloo. The Class 50s were drafted on to the Waterloo trains from late 1979 and their 100mph capability has resulted in improved timings over the route, together with the provision of some electrically-heated, air-braked Mk 2 coaching stock. In other respects, such as the reduction of train catering, the service has continued to decline. *Les Bertram*

Left: The only traffic over the remaining section of the SR Exeter-Plymouth main line is granite track ballast from Meldon quarry. On 13 July 1976 Class 31 No 31.209 eases a string of empty hoppers bound for Meldon down the bank into Exeter St Davids. *B. Morrison*

Exeter-Barnstaple Line

Length: 39.75 miles

The Exeter and Crediton Railway Act of 1832 authorised construction of a line from the Exeter Canal basin at St Thomas's to the flour mills at Crediton. In 1837 an extension to Barnstaple was proposed, but neither line was built.

It was not until the Bristol & Exeter Railway's broad gauge line reached Exeter in 1844 that the idea of a line to Crediton was again taken up. The new proposal was for a line diverging from the B&ER at Cowley Bridge. It was to be an independent line with a proviso allowing the B&ER to purchase it at a later date. This proviso was, however, rejected by a majority of shareholders, many of whom had taken up shares on behalf of the LSWR and had held them for less than a week.

The line opened on 12 May 1851 and when the LSWR line from Yeovil reached Exeter nine years later, their majority shareholding in the Exeter & Crediton provided a stepping stone into North Devon and Cornwall. Although the E&C line had been worked from the outset by the Bristol & Exeter the LSWR lost no time in taking over, installing standard gauge and operating the line from 1 January 1862. To connect the E&C into their system at Exeter a short steeply graded link was constructed between the two Exeter stations.

The line to Barnstaple — 39.75 miles in length — is one of the few surviving ex-SR lines in the West of England and its service is basically a dmu shuttle from Exeter St Davids. Nowadays there is little through freight traffic to Barnstaple, save for cement from Barnstaple itself, and clay from Meeth on the line to Halwill. The iron bridge which carried the Ilfracombe line across the Taw estuary has been dismantled and Barnstaple Town station stands derelict adjacent to the new municipal offices. The Junction station now has track in only two of its three platforms and work on improvements to the station commenced in 1981. Passenger traffic has shown something of a recovery with promises of improved summer services in years to come, while privately sponsored attempts to reinstate services to Bideford might yet bear fruit.

Most of the intermediate stations have substantial station buildings which are now occupied as private homes, while the adjacent station platforms are provided with bus stop shelter facilities. Services are operated by 'Pay-trains' with tickets issued on the train and most of the intermediate stations are now request stops. The curious little station at Portsmouth Arms which serves little other than the public house of the same name was demolished in 1980 and replaced with a bare platform.

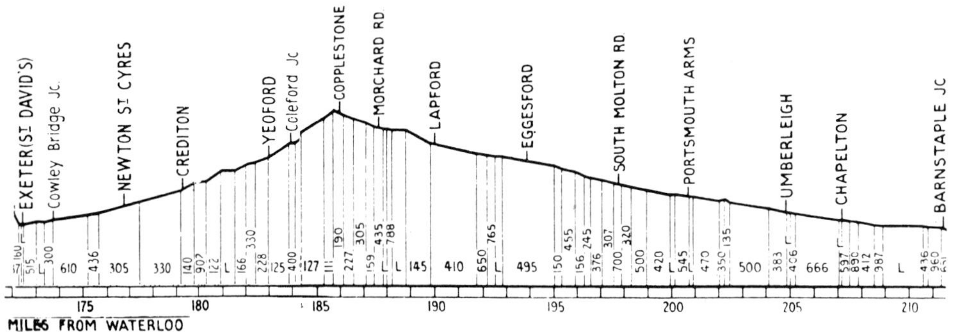

Bottom, far left: In 1976 there were more locomotive-hauled trains on the Barnstaple line than there are today. On 10 July 1976 No 31.117 had charge of the 14.40 through Barnstaple-Paddington train seen here awaiting departure. Even at this date, original LSWR timber goods sheds were a rarity. *Brian Morrison*

Top left: Typical of the rationalisation on the North Devon line is this view of the pretty station at Umberleigh on 19 October 1976. A Class 118 dmu hauling a parcels van calls with the 08.44 Exeter-Barnstaple in less than glorious weather. *Les Bertram*

Centre left: Attractive stone station buildings are a feature of the North Devon line, and Kings Nympton, now occupied as a private dwelling, is surely one of the prettiest.

Below centre: A flashback to steam days and a reminder of the complexities of the old freight workings. SR Light Pacific No 34083 *605 Squadron* waits in the yard at Eggesford with the 12.50 Torrington/15.25 Barnstaple-Feltham freight, on 15 June 1964. It is waiting to be overtaken by an up passenger train. *J. R. Besley*

Below: Lapford remains one of the busier stations on the line although most of the sidings seen in this view have now gone. A mixed dmu rake forms the 14.12 to Exeter seen on a very bleak Sunday in January 1976.

Above: Class 25 No 25.080 heads away from the deserted Morchard Road station with the 07.35 Barnstaple-Exeter St Davids on 6 August 1976. *Les Bertram*

Centre right: In the early 1970s Crediton station still retained some nice LSWR gas lamps as well as its original B&ER-style station building. *R. E. Toop*

Bottom right: Another view of Crediton, showing the nice LSWR signalbox similar to the 'listed' example at Instow. Class 46 No 46.002 approaches with a heavy load of ballast from Meldon quarry on 24 July 1975. *D. Griffiths*

Top left: Through trains over the ex-LSWR route from Plymouth joined the GWR line into Exeter at Cowley Bridge junction. 'Warship' No D826 *Jupiter* rolls the 10.10 Plymouth-Waterloo gently through the switches on a sunny 3 May 1964. *M. J. Fox*

Centre left: A more recent view of Cowley Bridge Junction taken on 5 September 1975. The now unkempt signalbox stands sentry at the single-tracked junction as Class 52 No D1059 *Western Empire* heads over the rebuilt river bridge with empty ballast wagons for Meldon quarry. *L. A. Nixon*

Below: Surely one of the quaintest and most delightful spots on the SR West Country lines was Luckett on the erstwhile Plymouth Devonport & South Western Junction Railway. The cottage with its adjoining goods shed and loading bay perhaps reflect the fact that Luckett had a greater traffic in strawberries than passengers. The 'board crossing' is a point to note for modellers. *R. E. Vincent*

Branch Lines

Exmouth Branch

Length: 10.5 miles

The Exmouth branch was originally intended to connect directly into Exeter via the South Devon Railway, but the Exeter and Exmouth Railway subsequently changed its plans and moved the junction eastwards to a point known as Exmouth Junction, on the London & South Western Railway. This resulted in a change of proposed gauge from the 7ft broad gauge of the SDR to standard gauge.

The branch opened on 1 May 1861 and was absorbed by the LSWR in 1866. In 1864 a connection was provided to Exmouth docks, but although Exmouth remains the only active port in East Devon, the connection has been removed. The Budleigh Salterton Railway which left the Sidmouth branch at Tipton St Johns, was opened through to Exmouth on 1 June 1903 and closed in 1967. Freight services to Exmouth have been withdrawn but a passenger service worked by diesel multiple units remains in operation between Exeter Central and Exmouth. During 1980 the Exmouth viaduct on the former Budleigh Salterton line was demolished to make way for a road scheme.

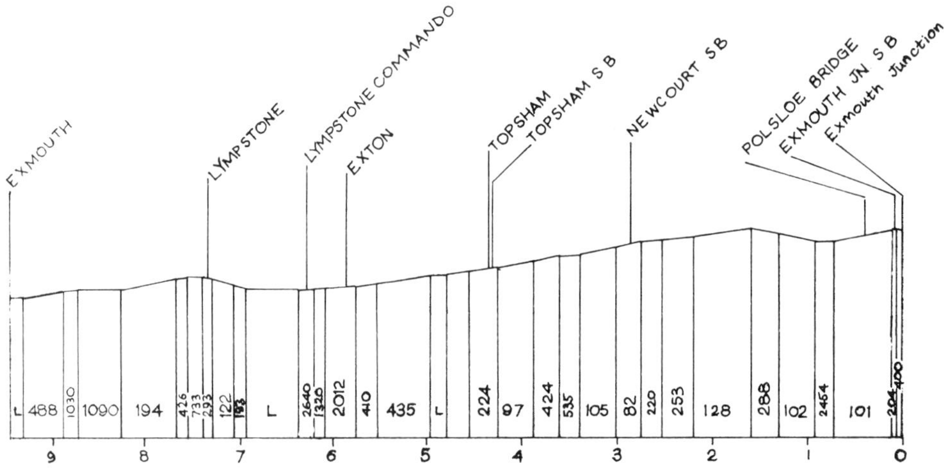

Bottom, far left: The rebuilt station at Exmouth provides only essential platform facilities as seen in this view of the 15.00 Exeter Central-Exmouth train arriving on 10 April 1977. *Les Bertram*

Top left: Facilities at St James' Park Halt are equally basic, but date from the Southern Railway era of precast concrete. *Les Bertram*

Centre left: A Swindon cross-country Class 120 diesel unit skirts the Exe estuary near Exmouth on 13 March 1976. *Les Bertram*

Below: The 16.05 from Exeter St Davids crosses the 16.08 from Exmouth at Topsham amid early SR surroundings. The train driver is delivering the single line token to the signalman. *Les Bertram*

Length: 14.75 (19.75) miles

The Callington branch had a most interesting and complex history, having begun as a mineral railway and later formed part of the Plymouth, Devonport and South Western Junction Railway. In 1859 a mercantile company promoted and built an incline from a wharf on the Tamar at Calstock to a point higher up the valley. Three years later the Tamar, Kit Hill and Callington Railway was formed in order to extend the track from the incline to Kelly Bray, but construction was halted when the money ran out. The works remained derelict until 1869 when the Calstock & Callington Railway took over and completed the line. By the time that the eight miles of 3ft 6in gauge line between Calstock Wharf and Kelly Bray were opened to traffic the company had become known as the East Cornwall Mineral Railway.

In 1876 there was a proposal to convert the line to standard gauge and extend it across the Tamar to join the Devon Great Consols mine at Mormellham, but owing to the depressed state of the mining industry the idea was dropped.

The PD&SWJR was incorporated in 1883 to build 28 miles of line from Lydford to Devonport and this opened in June 1890. The purchase of the ECMR was completed by the PD&SWJR in 1894, that company itself being a subsidiary of the London & South Western Railway, although the Waterloo management took little interest in it. In 1899 an order was obtained for a light railway of 3ft 6in gauge to bridge the Tamar and connect at Calstock with the ECMR, but nothing was done until 1905 when a further Act allowed the purchase of extra land and facilitated the change to standard gauge. Stations were provided at Bere Alston, Calstock, Gunnislake, Chilsworthy, Latchley and Luckett, and the terminus at Kelly Bray was renamed Callington.

The war years caused many Plymouth residents to move out of the city to the safety of the Callington &

Gunnislake area, bringing increased traffic to the line. Between 1950-8 the line was transferred to the Western Region for commercial purposes and then returned to the SR until 1963. It was then dieselised with a dmu working the passenger services and a Class 22 diesel-hydraulic on the occasional freight trains. The section between Gunnislake and Callington was closed completely from 7 November 1966, the rest of the line being retained because the viaduct over the River Tamar at Calstock provided the only easy access to Plymouth from Gunnislake and Calstock. This viaduct was originally provided with a wagon lift to convey rail vehicles to the wharf at Calstock.

The branch is now operated as a dmu shuttle from Plymouth serving stations in the Devonport and St Budeaux areas en route. The branch stations have lost their delightfully ramshackle PD&SWJR buildings of timber and corrugated iron, and now have the utilitarian shelters typical of most unstaffed stations in the west.

Top right: Gunnislake is the present terminus of the former Callington branch. Its original PD&SWJR building, roof timber and corrugated iron, derelict in this 1976 view, has been replaced with a 'vandal proof' stone shelter. *Les Bertram*

Centre right: A Class 118 dmu minus its centre car forms the 18.15 Plymouth-Gunnislake seen here crossing Tamerton viaduct on 4 October 1979. *Les Bertram*

Bottom right: The River Tamar which forms the boundary between Devon and Cornwall also forms a natural barrier to travel, and since Calstock viaduct is one of the few river crossings it provides the main reason for retention of the branch rail service. In this panoramic view of Calstock, a dmu slips quietly away from the village while working from Plymouth-Gunnislake on 5 July 1980. *Brian Morrison*

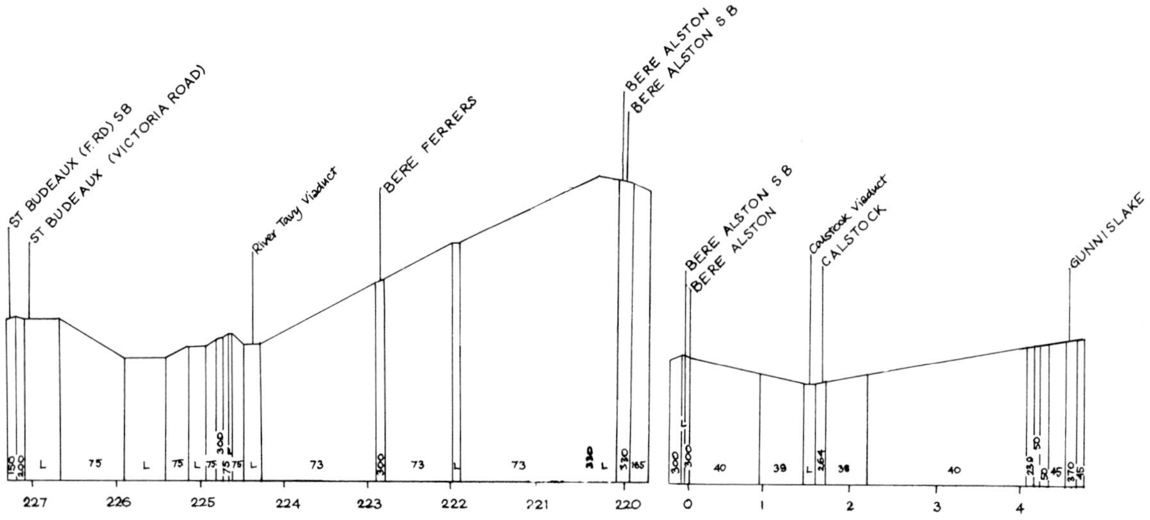

Looe Branch

Length: 8.75 miles

The Liskeard & Caradon Railway (L&CR) was authorised under an act of 1843 in order to replace the Liskeard and Looe Union Canal with a railway line between South Caradon and a point near Moorswater. It included a branch to the Cheesewring quarries and, indeed, the line was intended as a freight carrier. It was not permitted to carry fare-paying passengers and got round this problem by carrying them free of charge, but charging for conveyance of their umbrellas, bags and so on!

The first section of the line opened in 1844 and the branch in 1846. In order to carry the former canal traffic beyond Moorswater an act was obtained in May 1858 for an extension southwards to Looe harbour from an end-on junction with the L&CR at Moorswater. This extension, the Liskeard & Looe Railway, opened on 27 December 1860. In the 1880s there was a proposal to extend the line to Launceston, but this came to nothing. However, a steeply graded connection was installed between Coombe Junction, south of Moorswater, and the GWR station at Liskeard. This diverged from Coombe in a southerly direction and turned through almost 360 degrees passing under the GWR line before climbing into a branch platform at right angles to the GWR up line at Liskeard.

As the mines closed down and traffic declined, freight workings north of Moorswater on the L&CR ceased in 1914, the line being closed on 31 December 1916 and lifted a few months later. Passenger traffic had long been restricted to the section between Coombe Junction and Looe but on acquisition by the GWR passenger services operated into Liskeard. There were intermediate halts at Sandplace, Causeland and St Keyne (for St Keyne Well). Despite closure proposals in the 1960s the Looe branch has been retained as a 'socially necessary' route and dmu services operate between Liskeard and Looe, still using the steep gradient which involves reversal at Coombe Junction halt. Freight workings also use this route to reach the china clay works at Moorswater situated in the shadow of the main line viaduct.

Rationalisation of the branch during the early 1970s resulted in the entire station and good yard area at Looe being turned over to car parking, a new station with basic facilities being built at the very edge of the site.

Below: Liskeard goods yard on 13 July 1971 with NBL Class 22 diesel-hydraulic No 6338 marshalling vans and a string of empty china clay wagons waiting to make the trip to Moorswater. *G. F. Gillham*

Right: Looking east at Liskeard station as '45xx' 2-6-2T No 4523 brings the freight from Moorswater out of the branch station and on to the main line on 24 June 1955. *R. E. Vincent*

Below right: Pressed Steel Class 121 diesel railcar No W55026 passes Coombe Junction signalbox while working the 15.00 Looe-Liskeard on 5 April 1977. *Les Bertram*

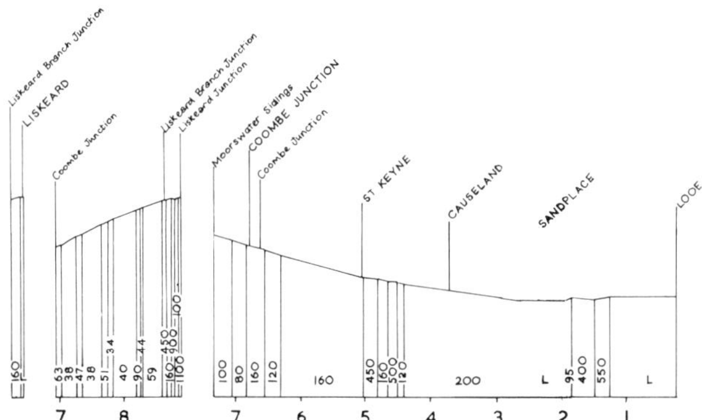

4523

LISKEARD
CHANGE FOR LOO...

COOMBE JUNCTION SIGNAL BOX
RIGHTS OF WAY ACT
— 1932 —
THE GREAT WESTERN RAILWAY
COMPANY HEREBY GIVE NOTICE
THAT THIS WAY IS NOT DEDICATED
— TO THE PUBLIC —
P 126

Right: The same unit stands at Coombe halt having arrived from Liskeard. The driver and guard change ends in readiness for the departure to Looe.
Les Bertram

Below: Looking north from Coombe Junction Halt as No 25.224 comes off the former Looe & Caradon line with china clay from Moorswater. In the background is Moorswater viaduct which carries the WR main line.
G. F. Roose

Left: A rural scene at Sandplace as the guard issues tickets to morning shoppers on 7 September 1963. *John Bourne*

Below: Parts of the Looe branch are prone to flooding when spring tides affect the East Looe River. In this 1976 view No W55025 clatters along the causeway beside the river with the 18.43 from Looe. *Les Bertram*

Bottom: The pretty little station at Looe was totally in keeping with the picturesque holiday village, but car parks were more lucrative than railways in the 1960s, and the rebuilt station with its tatty fence and basic facilities was pushed out to the very edge of town. In spite of this the branch still makes a splendid ride which visitors should not miss. A 1976 view. *Les Bertram*

Newquay Branch and Fowey Branch

Length: Newquay 20.75 miles
Fowey 5.5 miles

For many years china clay or kaolin has formed the principal freight traffic from Cornwall, and many of the early railways in the Royal Duchy were built to serve the china clay industry. The first of these was built by J. T. Treffry and included a canal from Par to Ponts Mill and a standard gauge line onwards to Bugle which included a 1 in 10 inclined plane and the substantial Treffry viaduct over the Luxulyan valley. In 1849 another line was opened from Newquay harbour to St Dennis, with a branch to East Wheal Rose mine at Newlyn East. Treffry died a year later and his estate passed into Chancery where it remained for 20 years until W. R. Rowbuck intervened. He formed the Cornwall Minerals Railway in 1873 and took over and upgraded the lines for locomotive working, reopening them on 1 June 1874.

The CMR system totalled 46.75miles including the route from Fowey-Newquay incorporating Treffry's sections, and Tocarn Junction via East Wheal Rose to Treamble and Gravel Hill. The latter section was removed in 1888 and part of the branch was later incorporated in the Perranporth-Newquay line. The Treamble section closed in 1917, reopened in 1926 and was subsequently disused although not dismantled until after World War 2.

The Newquay & Cornwall Junction Railway, opened in 1869, ran from Burngullow on the Cornwall Railway main line to Drinnick Mill and St Dennis Junction and was built to broad gauge. In an effort to augment its income, the Cornwall Minerals Railway opened its Newquay-Fowey line to passenger traffic in June 1876 and leased it to the GWR from the following year.

On 1 June 1869 the broad gauge Lostwithiel & Fowey Railway opened for freight to Carne Point, one mile short of Fowey. It carried china clay at such low rates that its income was insufficient to cover the cost of renewals and when its bridges became unsafe it was forced to close on 1 January 1880. It reopened as a standard gauge passenger line to Fowey on 16 September 1895. For a time it provided an alternative route to Fowey but on 8 July 1929 the GWR withdrew passenger services on the old CMR route from St Blazey, although it remained in use for china clay traffic until August 1968. Subsequently, part of the route was converted to form a private haul road for china clay lorries.

The Chacewater-Newquay line opened as far as Perranporth on 6 July 1903 and the rest, using part of the East Wheal Rose mineral branch on 2 January 1905. Initially a triangular junction was provided at Chacewater but this was subsequently altered to a single line connection. The line was reputed to have carried some 250,000 passengers annually during the 1950s but little of this was generated in the villages which it served and it was closed completely from 4 February 1963.

The Par-Newquay line remains in use for passenger traffic despite threatened closure on several occasions, but rationalisation has reduced the intermediate stations to unstaffed halts. The lines from Bugle-Carbis, St Dennis-Meledor Mill and Burngullow-Parkandillack and Drinnick Mill remain in use for china clay traffic. The Lostwithiel-Fowey branch remains in use for china clay traffic to the special transhipment wharf at Carne Point. Here, the timber wagons are tipped on end to deposit their load in special hoppers for transfer to waiting ships moored in the river estuary. In recent years the deteriorating state of these wagons gave rise to doubts over the future of rail-borne china clay traffic. BR was unable to fund the construction of new specialised vehicles to suit the traffic and it was feared that, as in the case of milk from the West Country, china clay traffic might also be lost to the railways. However, arrangements have now been made for production of new china clay wagons, so it appears that the future of the remaining Cornish freight lines should be safe for some years to come.

Top right: A Swindon cross-country Class 120 unit working the 15.16 Newquay-Par, passes under Treffry aqueduct near Luxulyan in January 1976. *Les Bertram*

Centre right: St Dennis Junction is the point where the freight lines to Meledor Mill and Burngullow left the Newquay branch. Today the junction remains in use for occasional china clay and refuse trains and there is also a passing loop on the Newquay line. On 4 July 1980 the 11.40 Par-Newquay gets clear signals as it approaches the junction. *Brian Morrison*

Bottom right: During the summer season Newquay was host to through passenger trains from some of the major towns in Britain, as witness the rakes of carriages visible in this deceptively deserted view of the station dating from the 1950s. *B. A. Butt*

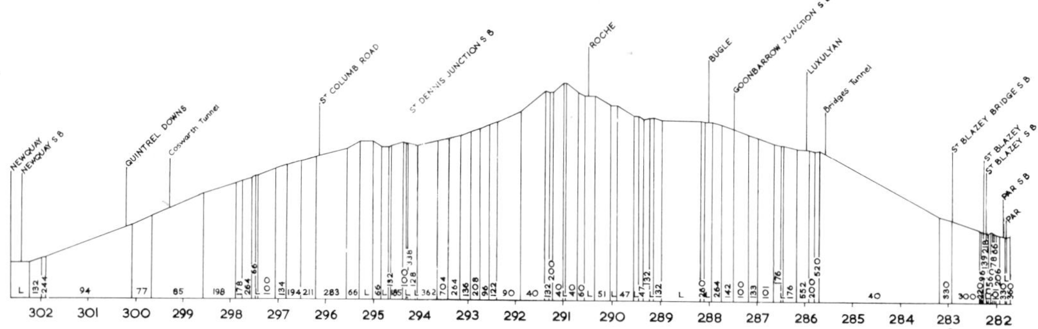

Above: A short freight destined for the harbour at Par is eased round to St Blazey by '4575' class 2-6-2T No 5537 assisted by an unidentified '57xx' 0-6-0PT. *S. Creer*

Centre right: Southwards from Lostwithiel the branch follows the estuary of the Fowey River towards the deep water quay at Fowey where the china clay is transferred to ships. This is the view ahead as '14xx' 0-4-2T No 1419 rattles the 18.10 from Lostwithiel towards Golant on 22 September 1959. *P. Q. Treloar*

Bottom right: The same locomotive was working the branch a year earlier and is here seen about to propel the 15.35 to Lostwithiel away from Fowey on 28 July 1958. *D. V. Cheney*

Above: The Fowey branch continues in use for china clay traffic which is transferred to ships moored at the special quay outside the station. This is the old passenger station in May 1969 while in use by English China Clays Ltd. *W.A.Camwell*

Below: The distinctive white-spattered timber wagons used for china clay traffic rattle along empty behind No 47.063 as it approaches the site of Golant halt on the Fowey branch, on 3 July 1980. *Brian Morrison*

Falmouth Branch

Length: 11.75 miles

In 1854 a contract was let by the Cornwall Railway for construction of eight miles of line between Penwithers (near Truro) and Penryn. From Penryn a separate contract covered the three miles of line to connect with the new docks which were under construction at Falmouth. The line was opened to passengers on 24 August 1863. Between Truro and Penwithers it was laid alongside the West Cornwall line although the two remained independent until a new branch junction was installed at Penwithers in 1893. In the same year, the Newham goods branch, which crossed the Cornwall Railway on the level, was provided with a direct connection into the Falmouth branch. The branch was connected to the privately operated Falmouth harbour lines in 1864.

The extensive heavy engineering works on the line included no less than eight of Brunel's distinctive Cornish timber viaducts. That at Collegewood, 318yd long and 100ft high was the last of the Brunel viaducts to be rebuilt, the conventional replacement being opened on 21 July 1934. Although Falmouth has not really succeeded in its aim of becoming a general port, it is important as a specialist ship repair centre.

In the postwar period the GWR introduced a through service to Falmouth from Paddington and well into the 1960s the branch carried many of the holiday visitors who arrived in the town each Saturday. It even managed to retain a year-round Sunday train service. Rationalisation in the late 1960s resulted in closure of Falmouth station in order to realise the potentially valuable site for alternative use. The branch was shortened by about 0.25 miles, the 'new' station providing the customary basic facilities. Subsequently Falmouth station has returned more or less to its original site, the new station being renamed The Dell. The harbour branch connection remains in use and the harbour was one of the last commercial operations in Cornwall to feature steam traction. An 0-4-0ST was used for shunting and even for assisting in mooring ships until well into the 1970s.

Below: On 22 May 1976 a similar unit forming the 17.48 Truro-Falmouth crosses Penrhyn viaduct. The ivy-covered piers of the original Brunel structure can be seen in the foreground. *Les Bertram*

Right: A Gloucester RCW cross-country unit forming the 14.10 Truro-Falmouth heads away from the main line at Penwithers Junction on 4 July 1980. *Brian Morrison*

Bottom right: The truncated Falmouth station as seen on 20 June 1969. Subsequently Falmouth station was removed to a new site a quarter of a mile up the line, but it has since returned to the site shown here, and the 'new' station is now known as The Dell. *W. K. Taylor*

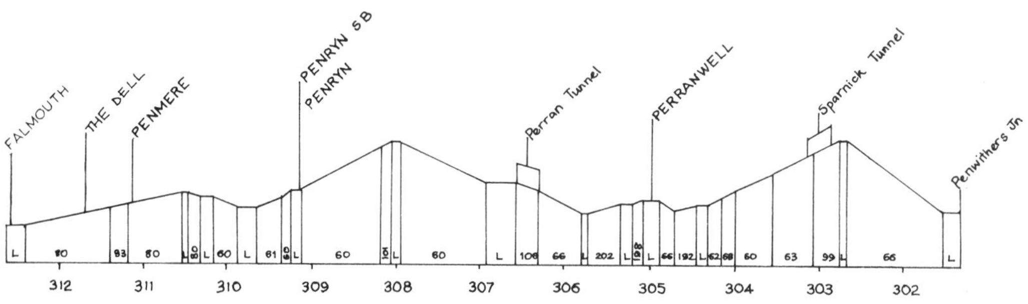

St Ives Branch

Length: 4.25 miles

The branch from St Erth to St Ives was notable for being the last broad gauge branch line to be constructed. It opened to traffic on 1 June 1877. The branch climbs from the banks of the Hayle estuary around the cliff tops, giving splendid views of this magnificent stretch of coastline with its golden sands and rolling surf. Intermediate stations consisting of single platforms without passing loops were provided at Lelant and Carbis Bay. By 1888 mixed gauge track had been installed as far as Lelant Quay. This was paid for by the Tyringham Estates on condition that if the standard gauge was completed between Plymouth and Penzance within 10 years, they would be repaid part of the cost.

In 1955 the branch was temporarily closed to enable reconstruction of the lattice girder Porthminster viaduct, outside St Ives. During the summer seasons a through coach to and from St Ives was included in the 'Cornish Riviera' express and on summer Saturdays this was expanded to a complete through train between St Ives and Paddington. The line climbs steeply away from St Ives station around the cliffs above Porthminster beach and it was not uncommon to see this heavy through train double-headed by two '45xx' class 2-6-2Ts and banked in the rear by a third locomotive as it left St Ives. The normal load on branch services would be two to four coaches with a single locomotive, spare vehicles being parked in the long headshunt at St Ives.

There was a small locomotive shed at St Ives with coaling and watering facilities, but the small stone goods shed saw only a limited traffic, mainly in fish from the harbour, and in latter years one of the two sidings was occupied by a camping coach. Freight services were withdrawn in 1964 and although passenger service withdrawal was proposed, rationalisation and the reduction of St Ives station to just a single track saved the day. Subsequently, as at Looe, the fine granite station was demolished to make way for a car park and a new basic platform was built on the edge of town. In the 1960s services had been reduced to just a single diesel railcar, with a three-car unit provided at peak times.

The St Ives branch story does not end here, however. Road traffic in the picturesque holiday village has always been a problem and the provision of additional parking places did not alleviate the problem of traffic choking the steep narrow streets. In an effort to persuade motorists to leave their cars outside the village a 'park and ride' system was introduced utilising the branch line. Large car parking areas and a new halt were provided at Lelant Saltings, near St Erth, and payment of a very reasonable charge allows a full day's parking and travel to St Ives for up to 12 people on the branch train. As a result of this, traffic on the branch has shown a dramatic increase, requiring the provision of four-coach trains in the first season. By the next summer the new platform at St Ives had been lengthened to accommodate six-car trains. The future of the line is thus assured for the immediate future and motoring holiday-makers are treated to the delights of a scenic ride which they might otherwise miss.

Top right: The St Ives branch was restricted to locomotives of the small prairie '45xx' 2-6-2T type and yet traffic in the summer warranted through services to Paddington including a Saturdays-only 'Cornish Riviera' complete train. On 4 July 1959 that working, the 09.20 St Ives–Paddington is seen approaching St Erth behind Nos 4564/71. A third member of the class will probably have assisted the train up the steep bank from St Ives. *P. Q. Treloar*

Bottom right: Many a happy holiday memory of St Ives will recall the sight and sound of the '45xx' 2-6-2Ts working hard up the bank from St Ives station. On a glorious day sometime in the late 1950s No 4570 heads away with the 11.50 to St Erth. *J. C. Beckett*

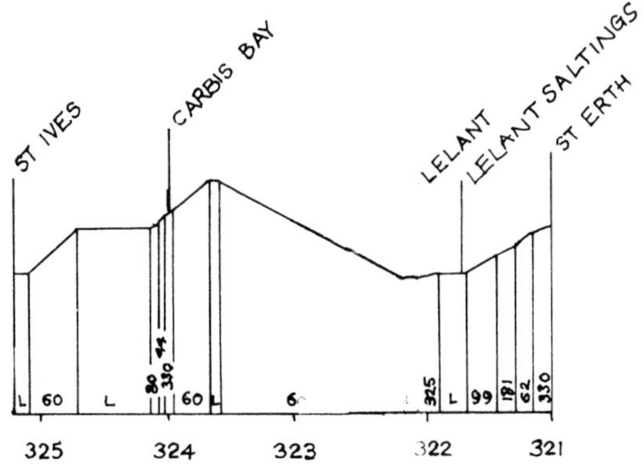

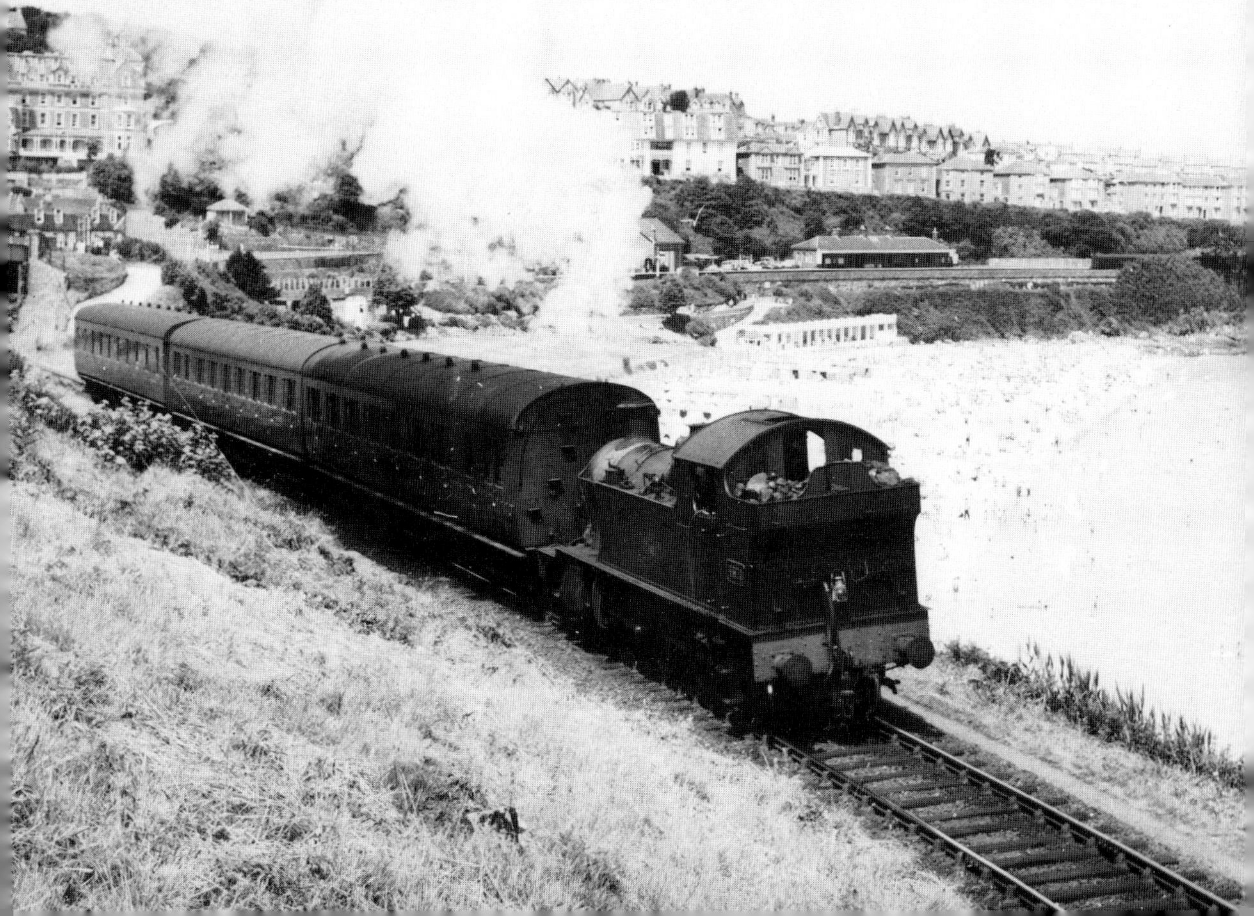

Above: The park-and-ride scheme injected new life into the St Ives branch and the single diesel railcar of the 1960s was replaced with a four-car train. This is the new halt at Lelant Saltings as seen on a damp 23 July 1978. *Les Bertram*

Left: The St Ives branch offers probably the best view of the Atlantic coast possible from any railway line in Britain. A three coach cross-country unit and a single railcar forming the 14.36 from St Ives ride high above the golden sands and rolling surf on 16 July 1978.
Brian Morrison

Above right: The little station at Carbis Bay which once had its name laid out in neat gardens on the bank opposite, has been reduced to an unstaffed halt. Clearly there's not much traffic in the offing for the train on 16 July 1978.
Brian Morrison

Right: Compare this view of St Ives station with that of the steam train working, and the grim results of rationalisation and the lucrative provision of car parking space are all too obvious. The fine granite station has given way to this cheerless concrete platform on the edge of town. Since the park and ride scheme it has had to be lengthened to cope with longer trains.
Les Bertram

St ERTH
P 557

Freight Lines

Bodmin and Wadebridge

The 12 miles of line between Wadebridge and Wenford Bridge was opened on 4 July 1834, initially with the purpose of conveying sand dredged from the estuary of the River Camel. There were short branches to Bodmin and Ruthern Bridge and the little system was the first railway in Cornwall to be worked by locomotives. It remained independent until purchased by the London & South Western Railway in 1846. The LSWR was looking to extend into the West Country, but at that time the nearest point on their system was 200 miles from Bodmin, at Basingstoke!

The Bodmin and Wadebridge remained in isolation until 1888 when it was connected to the rival GWR system by a line from Bodmin General to Boscarne Junction. It was not until 1895 that the LSWR's North Cornwall line reached Wadebridge and so facilitated easy interchange between the B&W and its parent system. Passenger services operated between Padstow-Wadebridge-Bodmin (North), but the branch to Wenford had only a freight service to a china clay works. Ironically it was the light axle-loading permitted on this line which proved to be the salvation for three diminutive Beattie 2-4-0Ts. The three locomotives, built in 1874, were retained to work the line and went through several rebuildings to outlast their sisters by over 70 years. Two of the trio are preserved, one at Quainton Road near Aylesbury and the other at Buckfastleigh in Devon.

Upon withdrawal of steam power, the passenger services were taken over by diesel railcars, while Class 08 shunters handled traffic on the Wenford branch. From 1965 until withdrawal of passenger services a four-wheel diesel railbus was employed on the Bodmin North branch, connecting with Wadebridge-Bodmin General services at a new exchange platform at Boscarne Junction. Passenger services ceased on 28 January 1967, but the branch to Wenford Dries remains open for china clay traffic. Freight services to Wadebridge were retained until 1979, being worked from Bodmin Road after the closure of the North Cornwall line. Freight workings to Wenford are obliged to reverse at Bodmin General and again at Boscarne Junction.

Below: A single wagon load of china clay is the only traffic on offer for No 08.113 as it waits to leave Wenford dries on 12 September 1978. *G. Roose*

Right: On 3 July 1980, No 08.954 was evidently much busier as it marshalled wagons at Wenford. *Brian Morrison*

Below right: A scene of bygone days in the Bodmin area as one of the long-lived Beattie 2-4-0WTs, No 30587, takes the branch to Wenford dries at Dunmere Junction with the then daily freight from Wadebridge on 8 July 1960. *J. C. Haydon*

Coleford Junction-Meldon

This section of line which is now retained only to serve the railway-owned ballast quarry at Meldon originally formed the middle portion of the LSWR route between Exeter and Plymouth. In 1862 the Okehampton Railway was incorporated to build a standard gauge line from Coleford to Okehampton. This was also the year in which the LSWR had reached agreement with the Great Western and South Devon companies over areas of influence in the south-west. Under this agreement the LSWR would go no further west than Okehampton. However, a year later the Okehampton Railway obtained powers for an extension to Lydford. By laying mixed gauge onwards from Lydford over the Launceston & South Devon Railway, the LSWR would have gained access to Plymouth but the bill was only passed when the clause allowing the LSWR to work the line was withdrawn.

The Okehampton Railway remained nominally independent and changed its name to the Devon & Cornwall Railway (D&CR) in 1865. Attempts to prolong the 1862 agreement failed and the D&CR became a subsidiary of the LSWR in 1866 and was finally absorbed in 1872. The line from Coleford to North Tawton was opened on 1 November 1865, and from there to Okehampton Road on 8 January 1867. The final three miles into Okehampton eventually opened on 3 October 1871. The route followed the contours wherever possible and the resultant railway abounded in curves and gradients. The summit was reached near Meldon, some 950ft above sea level and the major engineering feature was the steel viaduct at Meldon.

The line was scheduled for closure in the Beeching Report as it represented a duplication of routes between Exeter-Plymouth, the WR route being favoured for retention. There was concern over the condition of Meldon viaduct and its one track was taken out of use in the early 1960s, the section of line between Bere Alston and Okehampton, including the viaduct, being completely closed in May 1968. Subsequently, passenger services to Okehampton from Exeter were withdrawn on 5 June 1972 although occasional troop specials still use the line. Its main source of traffic continues to be track ballast from Meldon Quarry, destined mainly for use on the Southern Region.

Below: A 'West Country' class 4-6-2 has steam to spare as it rolls the up 'Atlantic Coast Express' over Meldon Viaduct in the summer of 1962. *J. Parsons*

Right: An unusual view in the quarry at Meldon with Class 08 0-6-0 shunter No 08.584 on shed. *Brian Morrison*

Below right: The remote and deserted North Tawton station is visited by the 11.40 Okehampton-Exeter on 12 September 1960 — a clear illustration of why such lines could not be operated economically in the 1970s. *J. A. M. Vaughan*

Fertilizer
Depot

Above left: West Country freight in the steam era — SR Light Pacific No 34029 *Lundy* waits at Cowley Bridge Junction with the meat train from Bideford on 16 July 1958. *R. C. Riley*

Left: A train of china clay empties bound for Meeth pauses at Torrington station on the remaining, freight-only, section of the Barnstaple–Halwill Junction line. Fertiliser and milk traffic were handled at Torrington, but have now ceased. *D. H. Mitchell*

Above: No 25.224 shunts loaded china clay wagons at the Moorswater sidings near Liskeard on 14 September 1976. *G. Roose*

Right: On 3 March 1981 No 37.206 heads along the single track from Burngullow with the 11.40 Carne Point (Fowey) — Drinnick Mill china clay empties. *C. F. Beatson*

Preserved Lines

Dart Valley Railway
Buckfastleigh-Totnes (Riverside)

Length: 7 miles

The former GWR branch line from Totnes to Buckfastleigh and Ashburton was closed to passengers on 3 November 1958 and to freight on 10 September 1962. As soon as the line closed completely a group of businessmen began the process of acquiring it for private operation. Although there is an active supporting Association of volunteers, the Dart Valley Light Railway is first and foremost a commercial operation, aimed at the substantial holiday market in South Devon.

The DVR acquired locomotives and rolling stock, including the distinctive GWR '14xx' 0-4-2Ts and auto trailers with a view to recreating the atmosphere of a Great Western branch, and the first train ran on 22 October 1966. Three years later, on 21 May 1969, Dr Beeching, the man who had been responsible for the closure of many such branches, performed the official opening ceremony and the picturesque branch was truly reborn.

Sadly, a road improvement scheme threatened the line and the Buckfastleigh-Ashburton section had to be abandoned to the A38 widening, taking with it a sizeable chunk of Buckfastleigh station yard. The DVR now operates southwards from Buckfastleigh for seven miles to a point just outside Totnes. The line meanders along the bank of the River Dart and serves a picturesque intermediate station at Staverton Bridge, winner of the 1980 Best Preserved Station competition. A new station has been built at Totnes (Riverside) but at present there is no means of access from Totnes town or the BR station owing to problems over the provision of a footbridge over the river.

Additional attractions at Buckfastleigh station include the Riverside Miniature Railway with a particularly fine one third full size replica of Lynton & Barnstaple Railway 2-6-2T *Yeo*, and a museum containing the South Devon Railway broad gauge 0-4-0 *Tiny*.

Left: The Totnes-Ashburton branch was a typical rural GWR branch line and happily the Dart Valley Railway has been able to preserve and restore much of the line's charm on the section from Buckfastleigh to Totnes (Riverside). This delightful view shows '45xx' 2-6-2T No 4555 crossing the River Dart with a train including the Pullman observation car from the former 'Devon Belle'. *R. E. Toop*

Above: Buckfastleigh station has seen many developments in recent years, some of them caused by the A38 road improvements which severed the line adjacent to the station. The footbridge is a recent addition, while BR Standard 2-6-2T No 80064 was rescued from Barry scrapyard and is here seen on test on 23 February 1981 after eight years of restoration. *R. W. Penny*

Centre right: Vintage coaches are a feature of some DVR services, and two examples dating from the turn of the century are seen at Newton Abbot on 9 April 1981 en route to Buckfastleigh from the Dart Valley Railway Company's Paignton-Kingswear line. *C. F. Beatson*

Bottom right: Another attraction at Buckfastleigh is this splendid $7\frac{1}{4}$in gauge, one-third full-size replica of Lynton & Barnstaple Railway 2-6-2T *Yeo*. It hauls passenger trains on the Riverside Miniature Railway. *G. & P. Kichenside*

Paignton-Kingswear

Length: 7 miles

The Great Western Railway labelled its Torbay trains 'Paddington-Torquay-Paignton-Dartmouth', but the railway in fact finished at Kingswear and passengers reached Dartmouth, on the opposite shore of the River Dart, by passenger ferry. The Paignton-Kingswear section was closed in 1972 by BR, but was acquired by the Dart Valley Railway which was already well established at its Buckfastleigh headquarters. The change of ownership was carefully organised so that there was no break in the services and the DVR, operating the line under the Torbay Steam Railway banner, simply turned back the clock by replacing diesel units with steam traction.

Alterations to the track layout at Paignton have enabled the DVR to provide a separate station alongside the BR one, and the double track line from Paignton to Goodrington Sands is operated as two separate single tracks. The former down line now serves the DVR, while the former up line is exclusively used by BR for access to its Goodrington carriage sidings. The first half mile of the DVR line is actually controlled by Paignton South BR signalbox. The DVR has a halt at Goodrington and an intermediate station at Churston, which was formerly the junction for the short branch to Brixham. Churston has seen much improvement in recent years since it had been reduced to 'basic' single track status by BR. Its loop and up platform have been restored and a turntable has been installed. The latter is a particularly important development since the sharp curvatures on the line produce uneven tyre wear on the locomotives and this can be reduced by occasional turning of the locomotives to run facing the opposite direction.

The line runs through meadowland and wooded hillsides once it leaves the seaside at Goodrington. It eventually emerges on to the riverbank to run along the Dart estuary with some splendid views before reaching Kingswear. Major engineering features include two viaducts and the Greenway tunnel. Holiday crowds produce annual figures in excess of 200,000 passengers and this means that some heavy trains are operated. The line is able to accommodate large locomotives and the DVR operates a GWR '42xx' 2-8-0T and a 'Manor' class 4-6-0 as well as prairie tanks.

Below: Kingswear station, now terminus of the DVR Torbay line, seen in 1953 with a through train to Wolverhampton departing behind 'Hall' class 4-6-0 No 4992 *Crosby Hall*. J. Lakin

Above: Dartmouth station, across the river from Kingswear, was linked to the rail system by a ferry service.
Ian Allan Library

Centre left: The Paignton–Kingswear line is suitable for large locomotives, and the ex-GWR '42xx' 2-8-0T restored by the DVR in 1978 was the first of its type to be returned to traffic on a preserved railway. It is seen crossing Broadsands viaduct, the major engineering feature of the line, on 16 July 1978 and has since been named *Goliath*. *A. R. Kaye*

Bottom left: The two DVR lines rely heavily upon the Torbay holiday trade as epitomised in this view of 'Manor' 4-6-0 No 7827 *Lydham Manor* passing the Waterside camp in June 1977. *M. S. Wilkins*

Preservation developments

At the time of writing several more railway preservation groups are getting established in the West Country with varying degrees of success. The Cornwall Railway Society has several small industrial locomotives in its care and these are operated or on view from time to time in private sidings at Imperial Dries, Bugle. The group has also acquired the goods shed structure from Lostwithiel with a view to establishing a permanent railway museum in Cornwall.

The Plym Valley Railway has established its headquarters at Marsh Mills near Plymouth and is proposing to reinstate the line from Marsh Mills to Yelverton. Its first locomotive, SR 'West Country' class 4-6-2 No 34007 *Wadebridge* was delivered to the site from Woodhams scrapyard at Barry in June 1981.

At Colyton on the former Seaton branch some one third full size trams operate over a section of the trackbed. Even the long-dead Lynton & Barnstaple Railway is now the subject of attention from a group which plans to acquire part of the track bed and to operate a narrow gauge railway over it.

Below: Although not a rail 'route' in the strictest sense of the word, coverage of railways in the West Country would be incomplete without mention of the Forest Railway at Dobwalls in Cornwall. This superb miniature railway follows North American practice and includes a magnificent model of the Union Pacific 'Big Boy' 4-8-8-4 as well as this perfect replica of a Denver & Rio Grande 2-8-2. *Brian Morrison*